CW01395750

PRAISE F[...]

"Steve's adventure reminds us all that wildness and countryside are never more than a bike ride away. You don't need to fly around the world for an adventure: all you need to do is step outside your front door, pedal out of town, and keep going!"

Alastair Humphreys

"Cycling from London to Pembrokeshire in just one week, Steve Silk is a great guide, enthusiastic and sensitive to the contours of the landscape through which he passes, and the stories and secrets buried within. It's a timely reminder that real adventure can still be found right beneath our noses, and a joyous rallying cry for middle-aged couch potatoes everywhere."

Mike Parker

"Relatable from the very first page, Steve's razor-sharp observations of human behaviour are as good a reason to pick up this book as the cycling journey itself. A historically fascinating, witty sojourn from the streets of our capital city right through to the tiny Welsh hamlets where Steve is welcomed with no Wi-Fi and an outside loo. A thoroughly enjoyable – and educational – read."

Rachel Ann Cullen

GO WEST

Copyright © Steve Silk, 2025

All rights reserved.

No part of this book may be reproduced by any means, nor transmitted, nor translated into a machine language, without the written permission of the publishers.

Steve Silk has asserted their right to be identified as the author of this work in accordance with sections 77 and 78 of the Copyright, Designs and Patents Act 1988.

Condition of Sale
This book is sold subject to the condition that it shall not, by way of trade or otherwise, be lent, resold, hired out or otherwise circulated in any form of binding or cover other than that in which it is published and without a similar condition including this condition being imposed on the subsequent purchaser.

An Hachette UK Company
www.hachette.co.uk

Summersdale Publishers
Part of Octopus Publishing Group Limited
Carmelite House
50 Victoria Embankment
LONDON
EC4Y 0DZ
UK

www.summersdale.com

The authorized representative in the EEA is Hachette Ireland, 8 Castlecourt Centre, Dublin 15, D15 XTP3, Ireland (email: info@hbgi.ie)

Printed and bound by Clays Ltd, Suffolk, NR35 1ED

ISBN: 978-1-83799-572-1
eISBN: 978-1-83799-662-9

This FSC® label means that materials and other controlled sources used for the product have been responsibly sourced

MIX
Paper | Supporting responsible forestry
FSC® C104740

Substantial discounts on bulk quantities of Summersdale books are available to corporations, professional associations and other organizations. For details contact general enquiries: telephone: +44 (0) 1243 771107 or email: enquiries@summersdale.com.

GO WEST

LONDON TO THE WELSH COAST – 8 DAYS, 2 WHEELS AND A WHOLE LOT OF HILLS

STEVE SILK

summersdale

This book is dedicated to Mum,
who we lost later that summer.
From her armchair, she followed every
twist and turn of my journey.

CONTENTS

The Journey

London to Fishguard

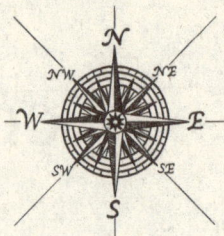

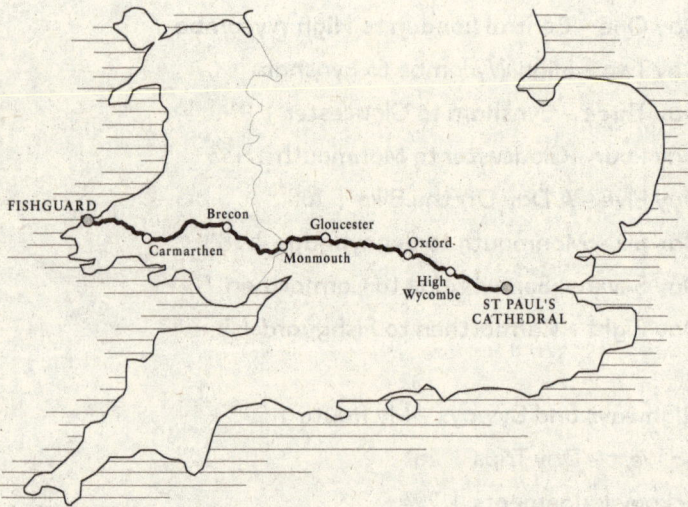

FISHGUARD
Brecon
Carmarthen
Gloucester
Monmouth
Oxford
High
Wycombe
ST PAUL'S
CATHEDRAL

← Direction of travel

PREFACE

A bellyful of beery laughter erupts in the courtyard as I walk the bike into the bowels of Gloucester's most historic inn. It's early evening and the after-work drinkers are enjoying the sunshine – as well as a good joke well-told. I'm equally happy – but perhaps more thirsty. I've covered 50 undulating miles in the heat, the sweat stinging in my eyes. Nevertheless, I'd started the day on the banks of the Thames and am now close to the River Severn – a decent ride.

I present myself at the front desk, bike helmet still dripping embarrassingly.

"Just booking in for the one night please. Oh and is there somewhere I can put the bike?"

"Another one?" says the receptionist, looking up with mock weariness. "Follow me."

We walk out to the central quadrangle where hulking great beams and galleried walkways loom down from all sides. The New Inn is a timber-framed leviathan of a building that has been welcoming guests for almost 600 years. It sags and it creaks, but still oozes an ancient charm. After all, everyone from medieval pilgrims to modern tourists have stayed here – they even claim a visit from William Shakespeare.

We head towards the back of the inn, passing a number of sash window shop fronts on the way – unusual for a pub and perhaps a little Dickensian, but somehow in keeping here. In the end, no one presents themselves in a top hat or calls me "kind sir" but you wouldn't want to rule it out. Instead, the receptionist scrambles for the right key and I wheel my precious cargo into a disused function room to find around a dozen other bikes laid up for the night – each one as dirt-ridden and as well-loved as mine.

We hear a lot about cycle tourers, those hardy souls who think nothing of riding 100 miles and then erecting a tent – a tent they have somehow strapped onto the bike, together with a sleeping bag and gas stove. Well, in the nicest possible way, sod that. There's a less noisy bunch of us who are happy to halve the daily mileage and double the comfort levels. We've been called the "credit card tourers" – perhaps not the most flattering of labels. But tonight, taken together, we're clearly worth at least a few quid to the local economy.

Either way, there is undeniably something special about a holiday on a bike. A holiday spent overwhelmingly outside with a form of transport that places you squarely in the landscape rather than behind a windscreen. A holiday where you *will* talk to strangers – just because two wheels makes better humans of us all. And a holiday where you positively deserve that big meal and a glass of something every night. I can justify every calorie of my creamy carbonara sauce at the restaurant in Gloucester – and I should probably have had another pint.

So come with me on as varied, as beautiful and as hilly a route as southern Britain has to offer. The New Inn provided my accommodation for the third of eight consecutive nights on the road between London and the Welsh coast. I used traditional pubs as often as I could, interspersed with the odd budget hotel and Airbnb. The inns provided the highlights – occasionally short of mod cons, but always full of character.

For the first four days I was on my old Jamis Aurora – a sturdy touring bike with a single pannier. With the help of some complicated pre-ride logistics, I then switched to a Voodoo Bizango mountain bike at Monmouth. It had even less carrying capacity, but its suspension and gears were better suited to the narrow lanes and occasional off-roading required – and indeed sought out – in Wales.

I roughly followed the line of the A40 – itself based on the old mail coach road which ran from the very centre of the city of London to Milford Haven. These days the ferries to Ireland ply their trade a little further up the coast at Fishguard. The trunk road adjusted accordingly and I did the same.

Fishguard, with its long history, rugged headlands and multi-coloured cottages huddled around the harbour, is a great destination. But it's the places in between that bedazzle and bewitch. The road passes through the Chilterns, Oxford, the Cotswolds, the Wye Valley and the Brecon Beacons. My particular route took in contour-hugging canal towpaths and a white-water canoe trip as well as Roman tracks over Welsh mountains. In the end, I realized I'd crossed three Areas of Outstanding Natural Beauty and two national parks in 300 miles – that's good landscape bang for your cycling buck.

Rather than camping gear, I packed books by an author who had cycled the same route in the early years of the twentieth century. Charles G. Harper is an important witness to that forgotten era between the demise of the mail coach and the rise of the motor car. He was rather conservative and quite grumpy – the further away from London, the worse he got. But I love both volumes of *The Oxford, Gloucester and Milford Haven Road*. As well as fine Edwardian prose, these heavy tomes include dozens of precise sketches. One hundred and twenty years later, the challenge was lining up his pen and ink "then" with my iPhone "now".

Cycling was easier in his day – even if the bikes themselves were more primitive. Now, drivers can be guilty of bullying the rest of us out of the way – even if they don't mean to.

But conditions are improving – albeit slowly and unevenly. Everywhere I went, cycle lanes had recently been added – with more planned and others being campaigned for. This kind of journey – my kind of journey – is getting less scary with every month that passes.

But what exactly is my kind of journey?

I guess it's the kind of slow travel that revels in the places in between. Exploring the kind of towns and villages that you bypass by car, but that you won't, don't or can't ignore on two wheels. And my emerging Law of Cycling Serendipity suggests that it's these locations that provide the unexpected highlights; the supporting actors who somehow steal the show.

At least, that's the best explanation I've got for stumbling upon a museum dedicated to the history of the photocopier, clambering up into a 2,500-year-old yew tree and being chased by a herd of dairy cattle across a Forest of Dean meadow.

The contrast with a conventional holiday couldn't be more stark. Abroad, in everywhere from Amsterdam to the Canary Islands I might be confronted with the problem of overtourism – cities that have somehow lost their soul thanks to the sheer volume of visitors they attract. Everyone panders to *them*, no one looks after *us*, say the locals. On the Greek island of Paros, protesters carrying a "Reclaim the Beach" banner marched against the proliferation of beach bars. In Barcelona, holidaymakers have found themselves squirted at with water pistols.

So setting out within your own country to explore the kind of places where you might be the only tourist that day, or even that week, has to feel more authentic and satisfying. Let's call it "undertourism". No airport, no passports and – thanks to pedal power – only the lightest of environmental impacts.

You might never be foolhardy enough to ride across the country in one fell swoop. But I hope that my journey will inspire you to get on a bike and go *further* in future. A round trip on one day is barely more than a commute. But going from A to B and then as far down the alphabet as you can manage, well, that's in danger of becoming an adventure.

DAY ONE

CENTRAL LONDON TO HIGH WYCOMBE

Day One

Central London to
High Wycombe

43 miles
987 ft of ascent

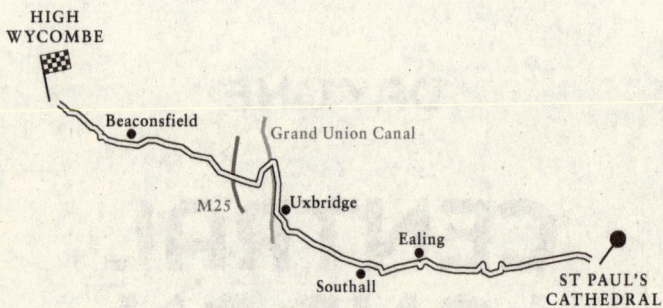

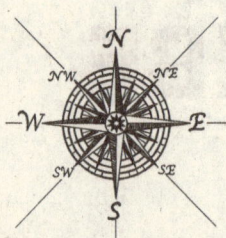

**HIGH
WYCOMBE**

Beaconsfield

Grand Union Canal

M25

Uxbridge

Ealing

Southall

**ST PAUL'S
CATHEDRAL**

N
NW   NE
W   E
SW   SE
S

Direction of travel

Amid the straight lines of high rise and high finance, the curvaceous profile of St Paul's Cathedral seems joyously out of place – out of time even. Throughout the City of London, you catch glimpses of this wonderful building from near and from far: God among Mammon; ancient near modern; Baroque stonework versus boxy glass and steel.

But I'm very much down at ground level, messing about with pumps and a pannier in the churchyard, engaged in the sort of low-level, pre-ride faff with which every long-distance cyclist is familiar. My bike is leant against the base of a statue to the saint himself. Us mortals are caught in the cathedral's substantial shadow, but Paul, atop his plinth, is high enough to catch a few rays of a weak sun. I look up to see him glittering in gold, his arm outstretched in blessing.

Does London have a dead centre? A place from where all distances can be measured, a place from where all journeys should start? Paris certainly does. Outside Notre Dame Cathedral you'll find a bronze marker known as Kilometre

Zero – which absolutely does what it says on the plaque. In this city it's more messy. A Roman era "London Stone" at nearby Cornhill used to do the job; similarly a General Post Office in Lombard Street and a courthouse in Clerkenwell – all long gone. Some say Charing Cross now has the honour, even if none of our major roads seem to start there. In that haphazardly British way, the A3 begins on King William Street, the A4 on Cannon Street and the A10 close by at the Monument junction.

But all I care about today is the A40 from London to Fishguard which gets going within shouting distance of this very spot. After much nosing around Paternoster Square and Temple Bar, I've decided that St Paul's statue will be my personal Mile Zero.

A bronze plaque will surely follow – in time.

Inside the cathedral, I remove my cycle helmet and drink in the sumptuous interior. The poet Philip Larkin called this "awkward reverence" – the moment a non-believer steps upon holy ground. Despite having all the typical agnosticism of my generation I still feel a pull, particularly in the hushed crypt. Large monuments honour military leaders like Horatio Nelson and the Duke of Wellington; it's harder to track down the smaller tomb dedicated to the cathedral's tireless architect Sir Christopher Wren. But yes, at the beginning of my ride, I plead guilty to seeking the sort of benediction offered by lofty acoustics and well-cut stone – if nothing more spiritual. I've paid my dues and I'm happy with my starting line. It's time to get going.

Actual cycling proves difficult; there are just too many pavements and people. So my journey starts with a walk down Paternoster Row towards a triangular junction protected by a platoon of City of London bollards. Funnily enough, if I took the right fork here I would be on St Martin's Le Grand and the start of the Great North Road to Edinburgh. By turning less than 90 degrees, I will head for the wilds of Wales instead.

I enjoy these philosophical "what ifs" as a journey begins. What if I just kept going? What if I went in a dead straight line? What if everyone had to go on a pedalling pilgrimage once a year; as much for the rhythm of the road as the thrill of the destination? Of all the hundreds of people in my eyeline right now, how many would fancy something as indulgent as this; simply getting on a bike and riding 300-odd miles from one side of the country to the other. To explore how England – and then Wales – change, subtly with every mile. To travel at a pace where you can notice the differences in accent, architecture and approach to life. To take the road less travelled and accept that, occasionally, it might leave you bewilderingly lost.

It won't be any kind of race – the point is to explore, to meander and to chat – however difficult that proves to be amid the anonymity of Central London. Perhaps the simplicity of the street names can offer some initial solace: Silk Street, Milk Street, Bread Street and Oat Lane. I love the historical transparency of this, the oldest part of the capital:

Old Jewry, Limeburner Lane, London Wall. My favourites are the ones that refuse to obey the usual rules at all. A short street next to a tiny park is called "Little Britain". And there's a thoroughfare called "Poultry". Yes, that one word. Poultry, just down the road from the Bank of England.

As I take in my surroundings I notice a pattern. Bemused tourists emerge from St Paul's tube station facing the wrong way, unable to see the cathedral. Three times, a bowler-hatted guide patiently gives them the "it's behind you" signal, the very picture of politeness.

"Welcome to London, madam. Yes, it's just over there."

I move on to Newgate. I could cycle, the crowds have thinned and the traffic is manageable, but I still feel as if *interesting stuff* would come at me too quickly. The ruined Christ Church, for example, its nave open to the elements, converted into a public garden. This is a place of worship twice destroyed. It was lost as part of the Great Fire of London, rebuilt to a Wren design and then gutted by the blitz of World War Two. Only its remains remain, a rough and ready monument to the pounding that London took.

A little further on, lawyerly folk spill out onto the pavements, clutching their documents and shooting the breeze. The entrance to the Central Criminal Court lies a hundred yards down Old Bailey, but the prison vans come in here – and I happen to have turned up at peak time.

The Serco driver waits patiently for the nod to drive into a subterranean part of the building. I loiter, keen to see the moment itself, before dropping back, sensing increased nervousness from one of the security guards.

"Well, you've got to admit, mate, you look pretty suspicious hanging around there," he says, not unreasonably.

From a more respectful distance I watch the van be swallowed whole, squinting hard at the small square windows – the kind press photographers haunt, trying to get a spectral shot of the accused. Who's in there today, I wonder. Is this the day of the verdict? Is the view out of that tinted glass the last they will see of normal life for a year, a decade, for life? And how many thousands of others have made similar journeys over the centuries.

Certainly, this neck of the woods has always been famous for crime and punishment. The old Newgate Prison was on the site the courts now occupy; people were once hanged as well as incarcerated within its high walls. Nearby, I find a sombre reminder on display within the seventeenth-century St Sepulchre's Church. It's the bell used to deliver the death knell to the condemned prisoner at midnight on the eve of execution – twelve rings outside their cell. The parish bellman was required to recite verses too. Among them:

Examine well yourselves, in time repent.
That you may not to eternal flames be sent.
And when St Sepulchre's Bell in the morning tolls
The Lord above have mercy on your soul.

I unlock the bike from the railings and decide to actually get on it for the first time. After all, I have a cycle lane, even if it's protected by paint rather than kerbed concrete. When you're walking with a bike, the mass of the pannier feels like a dead weight. Now I've built up a modicum of momentum, it's all more manageable. It's good to push the pedals at last.

On the road, to my consternation, every single cyclist seems to overtake me. It's only when I detect the odd high-pitched whirr that I realize a good half of them are e-bikes – electric motors taking the strain. It's technology that's changed since my last ride out from London, not me. Suddenly everything feels OK again.

The next feature is Holburn Viaduct – a cast iron masterpiece across another street below. I must have used this bridge a hundred times in a previous London life living nearby, but I'd never paid it any attention. Arguably, it is the world's first flyover, created to help the Victorians avoid dipping into the valley of the Fleet – one of dozens of rivers long since pushed underground. The viaduct slices obliquely, creating obtuse and acute angles for the ornate buildings wedged at the four corners, clearly an architectural wonder of its time. You can even argue that the reason we ignore it today is because it fits so snugly into the capital's contours. Topography often seems to be erased in Central London. Until now I've regretted that invisibility. Today I realize that I should probably be praising good architecture and great civil engineering instead.

My route above ground echoes the Central Line tube beneath. From Chancery Lane to Holburn we move from the legal world to business; from Holburn to Tottenham Court Road it shifts to retail. And Oxford Street itself is like every other high street in the country, less glamorous than it used to be, shabby even in places. It's quieter too, now that the morning rush hour is finally over. Even around Oxford Circus there's only a smattering of shoppers. Instead my eye is drawn to a scruffy greybeard festooned with biblical verses scribbled on pieces of cardboard pinned, held and hung on a threadbare corduroy jacket. He walks silently, the model of tranquillity, but you can just sense that he's waiting to catch someone's eye and launch into a feisty, open-air sermon.

Retail paradise ends, in no uncertain terms, with a giant road junction. In fact I am sucked into one of those uncomfortable zones where pedestrians and cyclists feel sacrificed to the whims of the motor car. It's particularly puzzling because, as a tourist, you might well want to have a wander. There's Park Lane to my left, Speakers' Corner on the diagonal and Hyde Park beyond.

The supposedly majestic Marble Arch lies in the middle of this interchange. It was designed as a triumphant landmark in the Roman tradition, but here it looks defeated rather than victorious. I retreat by the length of a few shop fronts, trying to like it, trying to appreciate it. I fail. From the east it looks abandoned; from the west, it's dwarfed by the commercial buildings beyond. In many cities this could be a central feature. Not here. Here, it's as if unseen giants are playing a game of Monopoly: a trifling monument taken from elsewhere and plonked randomly within the red buses, black cabs and careworn tarmac. Do not pass Go... etc. etc.

But beyond it, London turns down the volume. Bayswater Road is certainly less claustrophobic – trees line both sides and I enjoy the views across the untold acres of Hyde Park. Broadly speaking, the capital's eighteenth-century expansion reached out from here. As the population soared, large country estates were sold off in great chunks.

Alongside the grand terraces that sprang up in their place, there were hundreds of much smaller so-called mews properties; a cheek by jowl combination that no other city in the world quite replicated. To find out more, I turn right behind Lancaster Gate tube station to seek one of these streets out. In the old days, servants lived in the low-rise terraces of Bathurst Mews at the beck and call of their employers in the larger houses across the way. Typically, the women were in domestic service while the men provided well-groomed horses and carriages. The design of the houses reflects this – animals downstairs, humans up.

An entrance archway, next to a pub, screens its very existence quite effectively. This is a service road, *designed* to keep the lower classes hidden away. But oh, how times have changed. Despite their size, a mews home is now incredibly desirable, often changing hands for a cool £5 million.

I can't resist a good old gawp. Creaking stable-esque doors are long gone, but their replacements still look horsey, for all they are bisected by bespoke bookshelves. The dust, dirt and litter of everyday London are somehow banished. Front doors open directly onto the street, but pot plants luxuriate, creating at least the illusion of front gardens. For some reason every resident seems to have an oversized olive tree in an undersized container. I only see one sign of habitation – a lit Anglepoise lamp near a window. But you wouldn't be surprised if a witty West End play was being bashed out within its spotlight.

This discreet, well-mannered wealth would cause huge hilarity to any nineteenth-century Cockney given the gift of time travel. Back then, mews were seen as having uniquely poor living conditions. The average property had neither windows nor ventilation to the side or rear – purely to ensure that the lower classes couldn't snoop on their betters. It was perfect for the family in the Big House, but hellish for those living close to each other and an awful lot of horse dung. And that leads me to the reason I have chosen Bathurst Mews over all of its contemporaries. Thanks to a company offering guided horse rides around Hyde Park, this is the only mews in all of London where you still see these magnificent animals in action. Working stables amid residential properties – and a little bit of living history.

I arrive to find an efficient melee of mounting and dismounting. A child of suburbia, I've never quite felt comfortable among these snorting giants, but I appreciate the incongruity of what I see. Nothing here feels like central London, not the smell of the manure, nor the nosebags of hay or sharp chink of horseshoe on cobble.

"I guess it's our proximity to Hyde Park that allows us to flourish," says the stablehand as she prepares a horse for its next rider.

"Are they mostly tourists?"

"Some are, but we have an awful lot of regular customers too, particularly at the weekend."

She also puts me right on my assumption that Hyde Park Stables would be the one building that *hasn't* had to be converted. In the old days, the horses would have been in stalls – unable to turn around or lie down. So the conversion here is to help them rather than humans. Now they enjoy more space as well as the bridle paths of the park itself.

I head back, first to the main road and then to Hyde Park. I want to reacquaint myself with the writer in whose tyre tracks I am following, so I find a bench and pull out the first of his two volumes. Charles Harper was an Edwardian gent who explored the main routes out of London more than a century ago. One sketch shows him on his push-bike, wearing long socks, plus fours, a shirt and bow tie, finished off with a sports jacket. With a bushy moustache and a peaked cap, he has a jaunty, confident air – as well he might. He was probably one of the very few to have either walked or cycled all 13 of the main arteries out of the capital, ending up in everywhere from Penzance to Edinburgh in the process.

This section of the park is busier than I'd expected. And when I start to carefully leaf through the book, I attract the sidelong attention of an older lady nearby. Her gaze makes me realize that perhaps I am treating his work as something akin to holy scripture. Published in 1905 and slightly larger than the modern hardback, the individual pages are thick – halfway to blotting paper – and surprisingly ragged. The phrase "rough around the edges" fits the bill perfectly. Jolted out of my reverence, I begin to read it like an airport thriller – and my nosy neighbour happily goes back to her foil-wrapped sandwiches.

Perhaps she would have been interested to learn that Mr Harper was very excited by this particular road out of London:

Broad and straight and gently undulating and bordered by parks and the mansions of the wealthy, that traveller who should first enter London by it, could not fail to be impressed...

You must understand that I write of days long before the cyclist came into existence – the cyclist who can in these days mount his machine at the Marble Arch and, if the electric trams do not cut him to pieces on the way, come to Uxbridge in an hour and a half.

This was very much home turf. In a rare mention of his own life, he recalls travelling back to Marble Arch from boarding school on "the old three-horsed Amersham and Wendover omnibus-coach".

I have trouble squeezing the book back into what I now realize is a ridiculously over-full pannier and take a proper look around. Entirely by accident, I have stumbled upon The Italian Gardens – designed by Prince Albert as a love token for Queen Victoria. Its formal design contrasts with the informal nature of the people using it. Young children feed pigeons, noisily. An Egyptian goose preens itself, showily. A leotard-clad woman shadow-boxes ostentatiously – all day-glow socks and tattooed arms. A sight that would be very rare in my bit of Norfolk is taken as completely unremarkable here. A statue looks down upon us all – there's always a statue or a CCTV camera staring at you in London. This one celebrates the vaccine pioneer Edward Jenner. After the pandemic perhaps he deserves a rather grander location. Or at least a pressure wash.

———

It's time to get a move on – as much to warm up as anything. The forecast for the days ahead looks good, but at the moment my June morning feels as if it's been plucked out of early March. More than one city gent, I noticed earlier, was still wearing a thick winter coat.

I cycle on, past stucco-clad villa after stucco-clad villa. But then the restrained elegance is abruptly replaced by razor wire and public order barriers. This particular pair of semi-detached houses belongs to the Russian embassy; its white, blue and red flag flying above the door.

Those barriers have been needed in recent times. I've certainly been here when protesters have been hurling pro-Ukrainian slogans at the front door. But today all is quiet, the blue and yellow flags replaced by a new street sign, slotted in between Bayswater Road and Notting Hill Gate. "Kyiv Road W2" it reads. A calculated rebuke to the Russians dressed up as street furniture; nice work, City of Westminster.

The embassy building confirms that I've entered West London's diplomatic quarter – which in turn explains the armed police at a sentry box guarding a leafy avenue. I can't resist trying my luck and – to my surprise – I *am* allowed to walk my bike down the street called Kensington Palace Gardens, but perhaps better known as Billionaires Row. On my side of the road we get off the mark with the ambassadorial residences of the Czechs, Slovaks, Libyans, Japanese, Kuwaitis and Lebanese – as declared by more large flags.

I keep walking, but realize that I'm doing so without much enthusiasm. The security and the silence are rather unnerving. It takes me a while to comprehend that this is actually the most un-English of streets. First, those armed officers. Second, gated communities. Then there are the questionable architectural styles. Venetian-inspired? Italianate? Neo-colonial? I haven't got the vocabulary except to say that I don't warm to them.

Are these ambassadors any happier than the rest of us, I find myself wondering. Do they even know their neighbours? Do they get the trestle tables out for a royal jubilee or an Olympic celebration? Ridiculous questions of course. In my head, I take this as final confirmation that I am irredeemably middle-middle class; hopelessly out of my comfort zone amid mock crenellations and diplomat-plated Mercedes. As a result, I soon get bored, turning the bike around in a sudden U-turn. The policeman, wielding what I think might be a Heckler & Koch, gives me the once-over at such a speedy return. We look directly at each other and then quickly pretend that we've done nothing of the sort; a tiny gesture, but reassuringly human amid the heightened security.

————

Blank Street Coffee on Notting Hill Gate gets the honour of providing my first caffeine injection of the ride, on the grounds that there is a bike stand directly opposite and a vacant seat next to the window. My next eight days revolve around this bike, there's no way I am letting it out of my sight at the moment. The café has a strong neighbourhood feel, with staff on first-name terms with many customers and indeed their dogs, whose needs are met by a bowl at the door – the bowl I tipped and tripped up over, on my way in. To my surprise, it's already lunchtime. I always run behind schedule on rides like this – I genuinely don't know where the hours go – but even by my standards, the m per h this morning has been embarrassing.

After a suitably Notting Hill meal of a Bacon and Egg "Cruffin" – here in West London muffins are clearly allowed to make merry with crumpets – I'm back exploring the side streets; impeccably smart townhouses painted in pastels alongside exotic restaurants clearly on the same site as earlier corner boozers. The film *Notting Hill* comes irresistibly to mind. For all its cloying schmaltziness, the 1999 movie did a great job of portraying the district as a "village within a city"; up-market shop-fronts and "whoopsadaisy" politeness. I turn right down Ladbroke Grove and find Rosmead Gardens where "mild-mannered bookseller William Thacker" (Hugh Grant) climbed over the gate with Hollywood actress Anna Scott (Julia Roberts) for a moonlit snog. A quick look at the map shows that Rosmead is one of at least a dozen private gardens lying behind lock and key – hidden in plain sight.

These streets didn't always look this plush. Nowadays, few people remember the 1963 film *West 11*. Also set in Notting Hill, it's a gritty drama featuring a "London loser" tempted into a life of crime. At first sight the backdrop is the same, but a generation earlier it was a substantially poorer bedsit land. No longer. On Holland Park Avenue I find a very smart bookshop, more colonnaded embassies and estate agents proud to celebrate their expertise in mews news. But they are quickly followed by a roundabout so sophisticated that digital billboards use vehicle detection technology to tailor the advert to the kind of motorist driving by. Highly questionable on road safety grounds I would have thought – and personal privacy too. Happily, a bloke on a Jamis Aurora can go under the whizzkids' radar. But it is busy and you do have to be assertive as a cyclist. A chap on a battered 90s road bike takes the lead, acting as though he *is* a car and deserves just as much space. Doggedly, I follow him around the buses and the vans, close enough to realize that his handlebar tape is in even worse condition than my own.

The roundabout forms part of the next boundary. London: the twentieth and twenty-first-century sequels, if you like. Behind me, what Harper called "Stuccovia". In front, the eye-wateringly expensive Westfield shopping centre, opened in 2008 and expanded in 2018 to become the largest of its kind in Europe. This was all farmland until little more than a century ago. Only in 1908 were the fields developed to provide a home for first the Franco-British Exhibition and then that year's Olympics. The bright marble cladding on the pavilions gave it the White City nickname which quickly became official.

I'm easily distracted in multi-layered landscapes like this. There are so many chapters of White City life to research, perhaps the toe-curling exhibits from 1908 of village life in

Senegal, "Ceylon" and Ireland – real "peak Empire" stuff. Or the BBC takeover of the area in the 1950s, Blue Peter garden and all. I could even take an indulgent detour to Loftus Road – home to QPR – the team that I have rather erratically supported since the mid-1970s for my sins.

In the end I restrict myself to one small diversion in honour of an Italian pastry chef called Dorando Pietri. Pietri was the man who "won" the marathon at the White City Olympics. On a clammy July day, he took the lead at the 24-mile mark but began to tire as he neared the finishing line. In fact he was so dehydrated that he took a wrong turn inside the stadium and fell five times between there and the tape. Each time he was helped to his feet. The enduring photo shows him staggering to the line, accompanied by the clerk of the course with an oversized megaphone in one hand and Pietri's elbow in the other. Two other officials look ready to catch him, while concerned London bobbies bring up the rear. The hats, the moustaches and the granular black and whites of the image itself give it a very Edwardian air. Inevitably, the second-placed American successfully appealed – on the grounds that Pietri had needed assistance. But it's the loser that we remember all these years later even if Dorando Close turns out to be a bit of a disappointment – anonymous houses skirting the edge of a large housing estate.

———

The centre of Shepherd's Bush is decidedly no-nonsense and very international. Within yards of passing The Green ("QPR home pub, 2 for 1 cocktails"), brightly coloured shop fronts offer me Damascene Cuisine and Dubai Garments as well as the Babylon Pharmacy and the Kabul Gate Supermarket. We're in solid terrace land too. Street upon street march off north and south, the patterns only broken by the odd swatch of green space.

Acton arrives, with my first proper rays of sunshine as well as hints of its past as a self-contained village. A milestone hidden behind St Mary's Church tells me I've ridden 5 miles from Marble Arch. That's all the excuse I need to reward myself with a drink at The Red Lion and Pineapple – a lovely-looking boozer with windows peering out in just about every direction. The bike gets locked to the railings in a more or less empty beer garden and I'm soon sitting down with a drink, surveying the scene.

The clientele are the opposite of eclectic. Instead they're strikingly similar; overwhelmingly men on their own, drinking a pint, reading a newspaper and aged roughly between 60 and 70. I'm instantly fascinated. Is this a case study in loneliness? What would it take for one bloke to strike up a conversation with another. Maybe they don't want it. Maybe this is their one escape from otherwise busy lives. A pint supped not gulped. Articles curated into a paper, rather than scrolled through on a phone. I can't remember the last time I saw so much newsprint. With newspaper circulations falling, it almost feels as if I am witnessing the end of an era.

I'm a journalist by trade, but I'm not as good as I should be at talking to people in situations like this. And here, my hesitation proves fatal because, as I start to pluck up the courage, a bartender comes over.

"Excuse me, but we don't allow bikes in the outside area."

"Really, why not?"

"It's just the rules."

I huff and I puff. The bike isn't doing anyone any harm, is it? She remains unmoved.

I try the power of silence. She stares me out.

I describe the epic nature of my London to Fishguard quest. It cuts no ice.

"So, what are you saying?"

"We're asking you to leave unless you move your bike."

Speaking to the manager gets me nowhere, so I prepare to retreat, pouring the lemonade into my water bottle, slowly and, yes, a tad theatrically. In fairness, a subsequent complaint to Wetherspoons gets a decent response. Words will be had, they promise. They like people to leave happy.

The mystery of the solitary pensioners remains unsolved – probably to the relief of the old boys themselves. But my summary eviction is an indication of how we cyclists can often be unthinkingly treated as second-class citizens. "That would never have happened in Holland," I grumble to myself as I return to the outside world.

Acton now merges into Ealing Common which brings a welcome sense of space even if its green, green grass is tessellated into triangles by a plethora of busy roads. Later, near Ealing Broadway, I spot a sculpture called *The Rock*, emblazoned with the words of a George Formby song – "Count Your Blessings and Smile". This proves to be one of a number of references to the world-famous Ealing Studios which I eventually find – scrubbed bright white and with a vague 1930s vibe – hidden behind the terraces. But you can tell something's up even from Ealing Green where vast pantechnicons are parked up head to tail. Young men in hi-vis jackets (I don't spot a single woman) patrol nearby, while older ones decant film-making gadgetry into open-backed pick-ups with names like Barbarian, Ranger and Warrior. One firm has the strapline "We Turn the Wheels While You Make the Reels".

Broadways are now all the rage. The sort-of famous one at Ealing is followed by others at West Ealing and Hanwell. In between, I cycle past a lot of buses, takeaways and hotels. Hanwell announces itself with a 1930s clock tower at a key crossroads. It's a smart little junction – they'd call it Hanwell Circus if this was the City of London. And just this tiniest hint of civic pride draws me to the Clocktower Café which positively welcomes cyclists. One customer ends up asking for my Strava handle so that he can follow my progress towards Wales while the owner couldn't be chattier. His Millionaire's Cake is pretty good too.

My road now descends to the River Brent. This, says Harper, once marked the western extent of London. It feels utterly insignificant today, but to the right, a railway viaduct does a better job of conveying that sense of a boundary. According to an 1838 *Mirror* newspaper article the bridge consists of "eight noble elliptical arches springing from massive piers of brick upon a stone base". And no, that quote doesn't come from painstaking archive work, it's on display for all to see at The Viaduct pub.

I cycle alongside the Brent for a closer look and then, on my return, follow the river south – purely on a whim. That's going to be my motto for this journey: follow whims, be whimsical. The diversion is soon worth it. I'm close to where the Brent runs into the Grand Union Canal, built to connect the manufacturing hub of Birmingham with the capital. Here, the topography demands that the canal drops 53 feet in less than half a mile. The only solution was a flight of six locks. They survive; a watery and working staircase protected as a scheduled monument.

It's more of a dramatic drop than you might expect, with welcomingly different scenery too. On my side, a tall brick wall marks the boundary of the old Hanwell Asylum; on the other, what appears to be actual countryside beyond canalside ponds and the occasional lock cottage. I get off the bike and take a seat on a beam – the bit you see the boaters lean against to lever open the lock gate. I take a deep breath too, the air quality here is so much better – for all I can hear the M4 in the distance. There's something about the very presence of water that makes you slow down – one walker appears to have said "afternoon" to an absolute stranger, for goodness sake.

Heading upstream, a sombre-looking building looks over the canal with a bricked-up bridge beneath. This was once Asylum Dock, a side-arm where they took in coal for the boilers and sent out produce grown in the gardens. If *Peaky Blinders* haven't filmed here already, they surely should.

Just above the highest of the locks a man tidies his ropes on board an ugly hulk of a Dutch barge – much larger than the traditional narrow boat.

"How long did it take you to get up through the locks?" I ask.

"Oh, I don't know, maybe two or three hours."

"Two or three hours. Wow!"

"It takes as long as it takes. There's no point rushing when you're on the Grand Union."

Even in London it's possible to find these oases of timelessness.

I return to the main road as it approaches Southall. Colours proliferate – the brightly coloured clothes shops and endless stalls of South Asian street food. Spicy bites and cycling don't go together for me, but I do succumb to a cup of sweetcorn – "truly tasty sweetcorn from the fertile farmland" according to the advertising.

We cyclists are well looked after with a slice of road properly separated from the buses. The only trouble is that all of the action is on the other side of what becomes a dual carriageway – line upon line of shops with ever-changing combinations of retail and business. I'm sure I remember a Sherlock Holmes mystery where our man solves a crime thanks to his encyclopaedic knowledge of shopping parades. Admittedly his London was smaller, but I think I'd have trouble memorizing them all on this street alone.

I switch sides because I like the atmosphere: vans and taxis reversing and manoeuvring; ceaseless commerce from people getting things done. The smells particularly pique my interest; something spice-laden from a restaurant, vulcanized rubber wafting from a tyre-fitter's, the aroma of over-ripe peaches from one of those "everything's outside" greengrocers. You have time to think when you're riding a bike and with a sudden streak of introspection, I realize that I'm more relaxed in suburbia. Outer London ordinariness suits me better than inner city bright lights.

Between Southall and Hayes End I actually get some miles done at a reasonable pace. But my progress is checked by The Red Lion pub at the top of Hillingdon Hill. It looks historic and has a story to tell: a tiny cameo during the English Civil War when a fugitive King Charles I rested here for a few hours. Fleeing from Oxford, he apparently spent his time "much perplexed" as to where to head next.

I order my drink at a comfortingly ancient bar, the hospitality deficit from that Acton pub long-forgotten. As ever, I see my £2 as paying for a licence to snoop as much as the lemonade. It's soon worth it. On one wall, there's a copy of a historical cartoon from a 1950s newspaper, showing the worried-looking king disguised as a servant, skulking next to a bay window. The pub's low ceilings, inglenook fireplaces and ever-present wood panelling make it easy to transport yourself back to his era.

Uxbridge lies at the bottom of Hillingdon Hill. And for the first time on this journey I get a sense of "high street" rather than "through street". Is it the prominence of the church, the art deco nature of the tube station or an outbreak of pedestrianization? There's an eighteenth-century colonnaded Market House too, even if shop units have long since replaced corn traders' stalls. I lean the bike against a lamppost and do a quick 360. The panorama confirms it. I'm going to give Uxbridge the honour of being my first non-suburb; the first place that doesn't feel as if it's been swallowed whole by its giant neighbour.

To the west, the high street peters out as it descends towards London's frayed edge. There's a border to cater for every taste in these parts. The River Colne provided the boundary between the now defunct county of Middlesex and Buckinghamshire. (One old poster advertising Uxbridge showed a shepherdess looking across a stylized river with the caption "Across the Colne to Beechy Bucks".) Then there's the Grand Union Canal again – largely shadowing the Colne here, just straighter and kept under a tighter leash. And – slightly further out – the M25, raging incessantly. Most importantly of all, the landscape changes colour. Out go the reds, browns and road-greys of the city, in come variegated greens.

Perhaps in celebration, I take another diversion, heading north along the canal to discover a stretch that many people call home – a gently bobbing, moored-up kind of home. I'm cycling along a broad towpath, but it almost feels intrusive because both the path and pockets of the verge are requisitioned by boat dwellers. In fact I nearly run over a Labrador's paws, the rest of the animal well-hidden in one of these ad hoc front gardens. After some almost unavoidable gawping at a dozen or so boats I feel as if I have gained a voyeuristic insight into the accoutrements one needs for a Grand Union existence – a motley mix of well-used mountain bikes, small electricity generators and barbecue sets among them.

In fact all of life is here. In the course of little more than 2 miles I encounter two nature reserves, one outdoor activity centre, one rowing club, a marina and a yacht station. I guess they must all have road access, but from my angle everything appears daringly off-grid for this outer London/ Home Counties hinterland. There are also three locks including Denham Deep Lock where I hear the satisfying call of a cuckoo – my first of the year. Its cry is muffled and slightly more staccato than you might imagine. Perhaps a youngster finding its voice. But if I'm hearing a cuckoo, I must surely be leaving the Big City behind. This shy bird's signature two-tone is luring me west towards the untold acres of Middle England. Appreciate the moment, I tell myself. They don't get this down on the M40.

Bridges come in all shapes and sizes. There's a giant concrete construction carrying the modern A40, an older one for the Chiltern Main Line and an aqueduct carrying the canal itself across Frays River. Most spectacularly of all, there's the emerging Colne Valley Viaduct. The design for the low piers of the HS2 railway line was inspired by the flight of a stone skimming across the surface. Perhaps this will become a twenty-first-century design classic in time – despite all the controversy over whether it should have been built in the first place.

Photos of the construction site are hard to take from the canal itself, but as I head back towards the A40 I get a better vantage point.

"Eyesore, innit?" says a woman, unbidden, as she pushes her pram.

By the time I've formulated a considered answer on how I quite like the soaring ambition of major infrastructure projects but am less keen on the rising price tag, she's long gone.

———

I return to the A40 at the bottom of Red Hill, traditionally seen as the first sign of the Chiltern Hills to come. Unfortunately the road quickly becomes a dual carriageway. Traffic is heavy too. Round here, the school run seems to be the start of a non-stop, elongated evening rush hour. After a mile or so I escape onto a succession of scrappy pavements, unsuited to cycling, but safer than the alternative. Their condition deteriorates steadily so that there's soon only the tiniest hint of tarmac hidden, camouflaged and disintegrating beneath a generous double-sided overhang of nettles and brambles. On the positive side, I am getting out into the sticks. London is now very much behind me. At this point in Harper's journey, he wrote:

> The first characteristic Buckinghamshire view opens out, a view of rolling hills with suave contours, crowned here and there with dense woodland, sweeping down to sheltered bottoms where the yellow roads go winding away to picturesque hamlets nestling in their lee.

Yellow roads and purple prose? Well it wouldn't be the first time. But there again Mr H didn't have the M40 drifting in and out of his mental viewfinder. Perhaps it really was that idyllic back then. "Suave" even.

Harper also reminds me to start looking out for a particular species of tree. A tree that was once as important to Buckinghamshire as coal was to Newcastle. Reader, prepare to be delighted and diverted by the smooth-barked, catkin-bearing, nut-producing *Fagus Sylvatica* – the common beech. Beech trees are to be found throughout the county – and they were why this neck of the woods became a nationwide mecca for the manufacture of furniture in general and chairs in particular – of which more later.

Just looking at the dense, roadside thickets brings back memories. I grew up down the road in Maidenhead at a time when birthday parties were nothing more complicated than a trip to the Big Woods, with jelly and ice cream afterwards. The woods of choice for my parents were always in Beechy Bucks. Memories of precise locations are a little hazy, but they definitely included lumps and bumps to run up and fall down, plus waist-high piles of crunchy brown leaves. Without ever quite articulating it before, I now realize that for me, a good wood is a beech wood.

The road widens a little, giving me the freedom to properly concentrate on riding the bike. I don't give my 2016 Jamis Aurora tourer a silly name, a personality or a gender, but I do feel it becoming an extension of myself, part of my identity. It's no newbie any more; sections of the honey brown saddle are worn to a lighter shade and there are bumps and bruises from scrapes down the years.

I've never taken it to one of those experts who specialize in fine-tuning human to machine, but trial and error means that I do feel utterly at ease with its dimensions, its capabilities, its *style*. I glance down to check both the chain and the back cassette before self-consciously regulating my breathing. This bike, I know, will bend to my will at the flick of a gear finger or the lean of my torso. It's a good feeling.

———

Before I know it, I am in Beaconsfield, clustered around a crossroads with the most straightforward of street names: London End, Wycombe End, Aylesbury End and Windsor End. You know where you are and you know where you'll end up. Inevitably there is now a roundabout, but the junction is still on a human scale, not a Carmageddon one. Aylesbury End used to host a market place too. But this was replaced, as the architectural historian Nikolaus Pevsner thundered, "by a prissy garden and parked cars".

I lock the bike close to the prissiness and go in search of coaching inns. Beaconsfield was a natural stopover point and some survive to this day. But I'm gutted to discover that The Crown on London End has long since been converted into something less interesting. It was here that the notorious seventeenth-century highwayman Claude Duval played one of his best tricks. Seeing a farmer walk into the pub with a large amount of money in a bag, he bribed one of the staff to dress a dog up in a cow hide and drop it down the chimney into a function room full of people dancing. The hide came complete with horns, prompting shouts of "it's the devil". Gravity and fear did their work. As the dog ran amok, the highwayman slunk in, pinched the bag and stole away.

Duval – at least as far as legend would have it – was the classic dashing robber, charming to women and dastardly to men. Having been hanged at Tyburn – I passed the very spot close to Marble Arch – he was buried in Covent Garden, complete with this memorial:

> Here lies DuVall: Reder, if male thou art,
> Look to thy purse; if female, to thy heart.
> Much havoc has he made of both; for all
> Men he made to stand, and women he made to fall
> The second Conqueror of the Norman race,
> Knights to his arm did yield, and ladies to his face.
> Old Tyburn's glory; England's illustrious Thief,
> Du Vall, the ladies' joy; Du Vall, the ladies' grief.

All this alleged glamour means I have to pop my head into The Crazy Bear on Wycombe End – simply for a quick nose around. According to the author John Timpson, Duval was involved in a sword fight here in the days when it was known as The George. Crucially, he wrote in *Timpson's Timepaths*, the sword marks can still be found on the pub's grand staircase.

The tale of "England's illustrious thief" takes a bit of explaining to the ladies on reception who aren't, perhaps,

Beaconsfield's biggest local history buffs. In any event, even the swiftest of glances establishes that this place is no longer a pub, it's more of a late-night venue with moody lighting and bizarre decor. Stuffed animal heads stare out from all sides, chandeliers glisten and there are leather-clad walls and mirrored ceilings close to a "Moroccan souk" lounge. I expected to find myself in a different century to Duval, not necessarily a different continent.

What's worse, Crazy Bear customers are smartly dressed without as much as a hair out of place, while this crazy cyclist is sweaty, dirty and with legs covere Broad and straight d in a myriad of bramble cuts. More in bemusement than anything else they let me in for a quick blunder around.

Sadly, I can confirm that the current Crazy Bear staircase is modern and without a scintilla of a sword mark. That particular slice of highwaymen's history no doubt ended up on a bonfire during the last refurb. But nevertheless, ladies, I thank you for allowing me in.

Slightly crestfallen, I stick to a tree-fringed pavement as I leave town. The M40 sits just to my south, occasionally audible, occasionally visible, but no doubt reducing the traffic on this, the original trunk road. The Chilterns are now limbering up in the background and the road itself is starting to stretch me. For the first time in the day my body lets me know that it's put in a shift. Office Steve needs to be replaced by the lesser-spotted Action Steve for the next eight days – but some of my muscles clearly haven't read the memo.

Certainly on White Hill I am grateful to the work of the eighteenth-century civil engineer Thomas Telford. The map shows the enclosed black marks of his deep cutting followed by the open lines of an embankment – smoothing the contours in both directions. I presume that roadside robbery was much less common after his work was done. But I'm delighted to discover there is still a Highwayman's Farm to my right; ecstatic to learn that it's overlooked by Cut-throat Wood.

_____

I say goodbye to the M40 at junction 3 and fall into the valley of the River Wye – historically important for the series of mills scattered along its banks. In the nineteenth century they were used to make paper. And when new technology threatened to make many workers unemployed, this part of the world exploded in public disorder – part of the wider Swing Riots which affected much of southern England.

I do love a historical riot. I am fascinated by what pushes normally law-abiding citizens to sudden extremes. Poverty? Injustice? More than likely. But there is also a sense that once together, "the mob" creates its own dynamic, with unpredictable surges of violence almost inconceivable in any other situation.

The key day began just before dawn at Flackwell Heath where about 50 people mustered at the sound of a horn. Armed with clubs, pickaxes, crowbars and sledgehammers, they marched towards High Wycombe along my road, picking up supporters as they went – a clear challenge to the authorities.

Every detail of what unfolded on 29 November 1830 has been painstakingly recorded by Jill Chambers in her book *Buckinghamshire Machine Breakers*. Suffice to say that it involved hundreds of men and widespread destruction of what was then hi-tech equipment. Copious amounts of beer were drunk at pubs along the way. I strongly suspect that not every pint was paid for.

But the reason I'm now turning into a housing estate in Loudwater is that the mayhem reached its climax at Snakely Mill where the forces of law and order finally caught up with the now drunken rioters. Remember, police forces were yet to exist outside London. It was a hastily assembled combination of horsemen and special constables who charged at them – and got a hail of stones thrown back.

So, what's left of the mill? I can find the river on the map and evidence of some sort of mill race. But it's protected by semis on one side and industrial units on the other. After much traipsing down literal and metaphorical cul-de-sacs, I find a substantial building set within a small island. The mill itself may have been pulled down in the 1970s, but the smart house once lived in by the mill owner is still there.

I try to imagine the chaos and the carnage of the day, but it's difficult beneath the shadow of an overbearing M40 flyover. The mob apparently split into two – one group smashing up every part of the mill's machinery, the other engaged in a pitched battle with the horsemen. Halfway through, the men of His Majesty's Stag Hounds joined the fray – no prizes for guessing whose side they were on. A pitched battle continued for a while, but eventually enough arrests were made to break the spirit of the mob, the remainder fleeing in disarray.

Later the legal system went to work, but many of the death sentences handed down at a packed Aylesbury Crown Court were subsequently reduced to transportation to Australia. My interpretation is that everyone came to realize that this was an uncharacteristic day of madness carried out by otherwise ordinary people. Certainly in the circumstances and the context of the time, I think mercy was shown. But the consequences were still grave. Take the fate of 23-year-old Joseph Briant. He was charged "with divers other persons, riotously and tumultuously assembled together" with demolishing mill machinery. Convicted, he was sent first to a prison hulk in Portsmouth Harbour and then to the other end of the world, never to return. Most poignantly, the records show that he was a widower, with the dates of his 20-year-old wife's death and daughter's birth strongly suggesting that the former died in childbirth. Taking part so "tumultuously" would mean that daughter Jane Elizabeth would effectively grow up as an orphan.

————

Back on the A40, a beautiful, whitewashed milestone from 1744 tells me that I am almost exactly halfway between London and Oxford (26 miles to 28 to be precise). Later, it's not entirely clear when Loudwater becomes Wycombe Marsh, but the Wye is still around, and leads me towards the centre of High Wycombe itself, away from rush hour fumes, mostly along dedicated bike paths.

What I really need now is a hotel shower, but I'm already late for a meet-up in a pub with three Maidenhead mates. In fact Johnny, Hugh and Mac are my very oldest friends – from our first year at infant school no less.

Mac and Hugh also took part in my first cycling adventure. Back in 1981 at the age of 14, we somehow convinced our parents that we would be perfectly safe cycling to Devon, staying at youth hostels. In as much as we can remember the details, we believe we used main roads. I certainly have clear memories of the first few miles down the A4, even if the rest of the trip has dissolved with time into a distant fug of teenage japes, sweaty t-shirts and fumbled puncture repairs. If nothing else it's given me a lifelong love of bike trips like this – for which I am very grateful.

"I'm amazed they let us do it," says Hugh.

Now father of two teenage boys, you can see a sombre shiver running down his spine.

"Well, I reckon we were safer aged 14 than we would have been at 16," I counter.

"No girls, no alcohol. Just a few late-night Mars bars."

There's a short silence as we ponder the restrictions we place on our kids versus the freedom we enjoyed ourselves cycling-wise. I now do everything I can to avoid A-roads – despite that Red Hill aberration. So is it the levels of traffic that have changed? Or the perception of risk? Or the very nature of parenting?

Johnny, who unaccountably missed that trip, is more interested in my bike. He's a proper cyclist – as proved by a Strava profile picture showing him at the summit of the Col du Galibier – a Tour de France classic. He wears the proper kit too, and I know he'll be looking askance at my slightly shabby mix of GO Outdoors jacket and mountain bike shorts. Politely, he turns his attention to the groupset.

"So you're running a 11/32 are you? Nice."

I have no idea what my gear ratio is. I just know that the nice fella at Lowestoft Halfords switched me from a triple chainset to a double, persuading me that I wouldn't lose much in the process.

"Yeh that's right. Thought it was perfect for the gradient profile."

This blatant bluffing seems to pass muster.

The sun disappears and the temperature drops. We retreat from the beer garden to the bar. Around a table we fall into our comfort zone: old stories newly told; old gibes newly thrown and – inevitably – football banter. If any of our wives wanted summaries, we would struggle to pull together more than two or three sentences, yet two or three hours go effortlessly by. Old friends are good friends.

They head home while I cycle to a Travelodge at the far end of High Wycombe's main shopping street. The bike comes up to the room with me. I don't seek permission anymore, I just do it. It gets leant against the radiator while I crash out in the bed. A solid 42 miles has taken its pleasant toll. Both man and bike rest up to the sound of ceaseless traffic on the A40 flyover directly below.

DAY TWO

HIGH WYCOMBE TO EYNSHAM

Day Two

High Wycombe to
Eynsham

36 miles
1,577 ft of ascent

EYNSHAM

River Thames

Swinford Toll Bridge

OXFORD Wheatley

HIGH
WYCOMBE

Stokenchurch

N
NW   NE
W   E
SW   SE
S

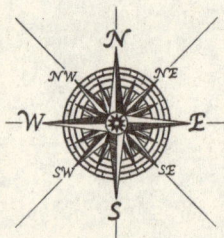

Direction of travel

If cycling has a habit of straining my back and tightening my hamstrings then swimming provides the complete antidote. And if an indoor pool can feel a tad claustrophobic, an outdoor alternative at 7.30 a.m. brings a lung-busting freshness that makes me feel doubly alive.

In other words, taking the plunge at Wycombe Rye Lido is pretty much the perfect way for me to start Day Two. The sun is up but has yet to impart any noticeable warmth. The water temperature is cooler still; "bracing" even as I get in, but fine after a few lengths. At this early hour it's all about lane swimming. You book a slot, turn up and select your speed. I've gone for "medium-fast" – a touch optimistically as it turns out. So I'm summoning up as vigorous a front crawl as last night's drinks will allow. But within minutes, yesterday's exertions are erased – like a bank manager writing off a worrying overdraft.

Back home at my local lido, I've been building up a mental picture of its typical patrons. It's amazing how much you can divine (OK, imagine...) from a bobbing head. Today's swimmers confirm my working hypothesis that the average UK lido user is female, about ten years older than me, steely of hair and steelier in manner; the sort of indomitable soul who didn't take any nonsense when she ran the PTA and has only mellowed slightly in the years since. Heart in the right place and all that, but woe betide if you cut her up on the homeward straight.

A child of the heavily chlorinated leisure centre era, I am a late convert to outdoor swimming. I first dipped a toe into this subculture as we eased out of lockdown – a time when only the most basic of facilities were available at the pool in Beccles. It was only when I returned in the summer that I realized the Spartan conditions were nothing to do with Covid – it's just normal life at a lido.

Today, I manage to stay out of trouble, complete my 30 lengths and pick up my stuff – part of the charming etiquette is that while lockers are normally provided, they are rarely used. Suitably invigorated – and yes, feeling slightly smug – I walk back to the hotel, the stroll giving me the chance to see High Wycombe from a different angle.

The lido is on the far side of a park known as The Rye. But calling it a park is rather an understatement. It's a massive breath of fresh air on the town's doorstep – more than 50 acres in all. Down the centuries it has always belonged to everyone – held "in common" as they used to say. After all, Oliver Cromwell had mustered his troops here during the

English Civil War – and successfully repelled a Royalist attack too. Locals had the right to drive their cows for grazing on its meadows until the 1920s, while sport, organized or otherwise, has simply never stopped. Head here on a sunny Saturday and drink in the activity, the life and the laughs.

It feels deeply permanent – every citizen's right. Yet in the early 1960s it came under threat from a council-backed plan for a relief road. What followed was a classic grassroots insurgency. The Rye Protection Society was formed, ancient documents brandished and newspaper articles written. The integrity of their open space would be defended by all means necessary. After 18 months David duly defeated Goliath and my route towards the town centre is immeasurably better as a result.

I walk across thick grass, heavy with dew, eventually reaching the Wye, clear, channelled and chortling quietly to itself at The Rye's edge. It's hardly the grandest of rivers, running for less than a dozen miles from the hills of West Wycombe to the Thames at Bourne End. But over the years, as we've seen, it has powered a lot of mills and provoked a few riots.

Now just one of those mills is in working order, and it's right in front of me. I first saw it on a Heritage Open Day when history was taking centre stage across the town. Pann Mill looks suitably quaint, but it's actually a complete rebuild, made necessary by the council's inexplicable decision to allow the original to be demolished in 1967. Still, the shiny black water wheel was successfully salvaged; its noisy clanks and cranks sounding pretty authentic as Stokenchurch wheat was ground into Wye Valley flour.

I'm now very hungry, but before I can sit down to breakfast I need to take a look at the town centre. Growing up in Maidenhead, I seem to remember us looking down our noses at our northern neighbour. But as I wander down the high street, I'm forced to admit that my teenage prejudices were grossly unfair. Certainly this place has the better civic heart. There's a beautifully restrained Guildhall for example – an open arcaded ground floor, ornate function rooms above, topped off with a delicate octagonal cupola.

Harper describes its wider setting as being:

> in a picturesque grouping with a whimsical octangular Corn Exchange, the ancient timbered Wheatsheaf inn and the tower of the parish church; while just beyond, the beginning may be seen of the amazing tangle into which the streets, having come thus far in a straight line, now proceed to tie themselves.

High Wycombe remains picturesque here and the corn exchange – more correctly known as the Little Market House – grows ever more whimsical. I enjoy reading the poster setting out the prices for stallholders as laid out by the "Chepping Wycombe Improvement Act of 1874". Elsewhere, the church stands firm but The Wheatsheaf is an all but boarded-up former clothes shop. And those tangled streets presumably lie under the Eden Shopping Centre just beyond a flyover and my Travelodge.

After breakfast, I head for the post office. Just one day on the road has convinced me that I'm carrying too much. The Day One maps get bundled up with some clothes and a couple of books – all deemed surplus to my streamlined requirements. It costs a few quid, but the pannier now looks less like a fully inflated party balloon.

I find the process curiously cathartic – and I feel ready for life on the road.

High Wycombe subtly changes character to the west of the town centre. To my right, on the higher ground, it's residential, to my left, more commercial, sloping down to an unseen river. This was once the heartland of the town's main industry – chair-making. Many hundreds of people once earned a living with wood: sawing, turning, bending, trimming, staining, polishing and assembling – transforming raw material to finished product with extraordinary efficiency.

Those days have departed, but many of the distinctive buildings remain – occasionally lying empty, but more often re-purposed. In summary they are small in scale, two-storeyed, well-windowed and with the staircases on the outside – the latter to help manoeuvre large items in and out. Once you've got your eye in, you can spot them almost everywhere.

Today, just to escape the West Wycombe Road traffic, I find myself cycling down Abercromby Avenue.

Almost immediately, I come across a good example of a former factory on the corner of Lindsay Avenue. A quick Google suggests that this one belonged to James Christopher Lane Ltd; a purveyor of dining and fireside chairs between 1907 and 1976. What's more it's one of *thirteen* furniture factories to have existed on this road alone.

I guess that helps indicate both the scale of the industry and its longevity. Even by 1875, High Wycombe was the country's undisputed chair capital, turning out an incredible 1.5 million per year. Why here? Well, the abundance of beech ("the Buckinghamshire weed") was one reason, but so was the resourcefulness of its inhabitants and their proximity to London. They certainly rode the population boom created by the Industrial Revolution. All those new terraced houses needed chairs. All those new schools needed desks and benches. High Wycombe was happy to oblige. Everyone's favourite photo of the time – proudly displayed at Wycombe Museum – shows a scarily high triumphal arch created from hundreds of wooden chairs somehow bound together. Built to mark Queen Victoria's visit in 1877, it looks pretty rickety. Presumably the risk assessment was stricter for another huge Chair Arch created to greet the millennium more than a century later.

———

If it wasn't entirely clear when I'd crossed into High Wycombe from the east, the delineation to the west is sharp and exact. I reach the Pedestal Roundabout to find suburbia falling away in favour of white picket fences and farmland. On the bike, the pannier is noticeably lighter and the ride smoother. Everything is less frenetic than yesterday's start in Central London. In fact my first village is almost a museum piece – the somnolent settlement of West Wycombe where just about every building is owned by the National Trust.

The trust owns the village because it owns the West Wycombe estate, once home to the eighteenth-century dilettante Sir Francis Dashwood – and still lived in by his descendants. Dashwood had a name worthy of a Blackadder cad and lived up to that billing in real life. He was an MP and a short-lived Chancellor of the Exchequer, but history remembers him as the founder of a notorious men's club that met at caves nearby. Were they just a group of toffs who liked a drink, or were there prostitutes and satanic rituals too? We'll probably never know, but even the estate's own website concedes that "free love and heavy drinking did most definitely take place". Blimey.

Overlooking the estate and the Hellfire Caves – now a tourist attraction in their own right – a hexagonal monument looms. It's a vast mausoleum, built to house the ashes of the Dashwoods down the ages; hideously ugly and grandiloquent. One Tripadvisor reviewer put it well, saying "it's like the setting for the cover of the album Black Sabbath never made".

Back on the road, steep hills crowd in. The A40 is rather narrow for cyclists and drivers to share, but I'm hoping to make the most of older fragments – some little more than lay-bys. The first of these contains the hamlet of Piddington, only created when another of the area's furniture tycoons built a factory here from scratch in 1903. Part of that complex – obeying all the storey/window/staircase rules – is still used for its original purpose, albeit by a different company.

"What do you guys make these days?" I ask a worker heading out for a breather.

"I guess you'd call it high-end office furniture," he replies.

"Expensive?"

"You could say that."

Piddington is also the place where the traveller must confront the Chiltern Hills in all their glory. Over the centuries, humankind has come up with a variety of strategies to deal with the climb. Most recently, in the 1970s, modern machinery blasted its way through what is called the Stokenchurch Gap to secure a route for the M40. Sweeping and swooping, you may recognize it from the opening titles of the TV comedy *The Vicar of Dibley*.

From my position next to the Dashwood Roadhouse, I can see the previous effort, a 1920s cutting which removed the worst, but by no means all of the gradient. Whenever I take this route by car I find a kind of permanent autumn within its shady confines – several seasons worth of paper-thin leaves lying on steep-sided banks. This was also impressive engineering in its day – and it's good enough to carry the A40 to this day.

Then there's the turnpike route going directly over the ridge with about a one in ten gradient. I've done this previously too – by bike. It's genuinely quiet – you might get the odd driver heading out for a dog-walk, nothing more. At the turn of the twentieth century – when brakes were much less effective – cyclists going the other way needed to approach with caution. Back then every serious rider carried a copy of the *Cyclists' Touring Club Gazetteer* with them. A copy of the 1897 edition is still available to be leafed through in the British Library. Its thoroughness is extraordinary. Every mile of "Route 37 London to Milford" is accounted for, both in the severity of its gradients and the condition of the surface. Dashwood Hill is the first on my route to feature the feathered arrow symbol – a warning that in those days descending by bike was too dangerous. It had a reputation in the coaching era too. The worst accident saw a driverless timber wagon – with four horses still in harness – career down the hill before smashing into an oncoming stagecoach. Amazingly no one died but, according to Harper, a lady was thrown out of the carriage "and one of the wagon-wheels literally cut one of her cheeks off".

I can hardly take the M40, but in the end I also ignore the A40 and the turnpike. Just to be perverse I'm taking a fourth route – one that goes back even further in time. I veer to the north and take a pot-holed bridleway heading gently uphill towards that wooded summit. On the very edge of the woods, a path rapidly becomes sunken within the wider landscape. Believe it or not, this was part of a medieval track between London and Oxford – and perhaps a Roman one before that.

It's a spectacular example of a holloway – a cutting in its own way I guess, but one trodden lower by century upon century of cattle being driven to market. I find the deserted setting quite magical. The deep brown of the mulch contrasts with the luminous green of the moss. Much as the steep banks mean the trees show their roots, the geology is in-your-face too. Creamy mounds reveal themselves to be chalky outcrops while individual flints lie strewn across the path like oversized pebbles from Hansel and Gretel. Squirrels scamper playfully along the top of the banks; the only human element, the faint whiff of burning brake pad drifting across from the A40.

But I'm a cyclist rather than a walker so I retreat to the winding bridleway. Thick mud, once gloopy, has baked hard, the rugged imprints of tractor tyres making the ride lumpy. It's a decent enough day, but there's not a soul to be seen. At one point, on autopilot, I reach down to adjust the suspension before remembering that option only exists on my mountain bike. I'd better just put up with the constant juddering then. That – and a succession of blue tits twittering around newly created nests – provide the only sounds.

The track heads towards Bottom Wood – one of the places where timber for those Wycombe factories used to be harvested. We can be absolutely sure of that because many of the so-called saw pits survive. Pre-mechanization, a saw pit was the only way that people could convert a tree trunk into planked wood. The trunk was hauled over the dug hole, with one man underneath and the other balanced on top. The top dog held one end of a huge saw while the underdog kept hold of the other – soon finding himself up to his knees in sawdust.

History manifest in the landscape, what's not to like? Perhaps a century's worth of disuse has reduced the depth of the first pit I come across, but it's still there, still recognisably man-made. I find myself squatting on my haunches, taking it all in. Trees have recently been felled a little further on, leaving an ambient smell somewhere between "sawdust" and "autumn". All well worth savouring.

Elsewhere in these Chiltern glades, so-called bodgers would once have been at work. These were the people who converted younger boughs into round chair legs with the help of a wedge and a mallet. Bodgers – like sawyers – worked outside rather than in a workshop. They would set up a camp – something makeshift for the men, something more solid to keep wood dry. Timber in all its forms would have surrounded them: the living trees of course, but also their dead harvest; stored logs, roughly shaped legs as well as branch, brush and twig. Photos from the time paint a picture of charming impermanence. The men would effectively take a stand of trees on loan, stay until their work was done and move on. Another wood, another dappled slope. I realize I am getting dewy-eyed when the hours were long and the pay piecework, but as I conjure up a vision of a fire burning and the lad getting another round of teas in, I can think of a lot worse working conditions in nineteenth-century England.

I begin to walk the bike up the hill towards the road. Halfway along I startle a deer, probably a roe, certainly larger than the muntjac and Chinese water deer that I'm used to on the Norfolk Broads. Then I come almost face to face with its fawn, wide-eyed in panic. Thankfully mum comes crashing back to show the youngster a way out of danger.

I rejoin the twenty-first century some moments later when my path meets the old turnpike road on the outskirts of Studley Green. This hamlet turns out to be typical of the small settlements that I encounter for the rest of the day. Smart white fences on either side of the road announce their arrival and as I cycle out, I'm normally left with an "oh, was that it?" feeling. Studley Green, to be fair, used to boast two pubs. One, now demolished, hit the headlines during the drought of 1921 when firefighters ran out of water and had to use beer to dowse the flames instead.

Of course there's no village shop for the chocolate fix I crave, so I head to Chris's Café – a traditional truck stop in a very non-traditional setting. From the menu, I resist the £10.25 Belly Buster in favour of a more manageable Four Item Breakfast. It's not quite lunchtime and yes, this is my second of the day. But there again on trips like this I could happily have some sort of fry-up first thing, another mid-morning and a third at perhaps 3 p.m. Food is fuel and I've got to keep this stomach well-stoked for the miles ahead.

Plenty of others are tucking in at Chris's, but I fail to make any friends. The chap I am sharing a table with politely rebuffs my advances, as does another across the way. Lorry drivers do a solitary job for a reason, I conclude. It's nothing to do with the fact that I'm on a bike. In any case it's happening as a decent episode of *Bargain Hunt* is approaching its hammer-down climax. We're all glued. Breakfast arrives with "squeak" as one of the four items. I've always called it bubble and speak, but either way I'm a firm believer that this heavenly mixture of fried mashed potato and unidentifiable greens is for life rather than just for Christmas. Like the truckers, I leave well-nourished for the rest of the day.

———

My route now climbs steadily towards the larger settlement of Stokenchurch which Harper describes as being "on a scrubby stretch of common land, very high and very bleak".

Its only previous claim to fame in my eyes was that a lad from our school lived here and introduced me to an obscure new band called The Smiths. What's more, his source was impeccable – the cool older brother Who Actually Went to Gigs. Thanks, Michael Elliot.

I'd hoped to get rather more under the skin of the place some 40 years later, but fall short. Stokenchurch lies directly on the A40, but its lack of an obvious centre is perturbing. Perhaps an old coaching inn called The King's Hotel once provided the focus. But as I cycle past, it lies boarded up – gutted by a 2021 fire. And I do mean gutted. Burnt roof timbers point skywards, unprotected from the elements. A dormer window, possibly part of a mansard roof, remains staved in. Perhaps it was unlucky with the fire, but it now appears unloved in the aftermath.

In other places the church would provide an alternative centre of gravity, but St Peter and St Paul's couldn't be more hidden away. I persevere to find a pretty sorrowful building, faced with some sort of pebbledash and topped off with a basic-looking wooden tower.

It all adds to a theory that's been building in my head since High Wycombe. This part of the world is pretty prosperous according to the statistics, yet I'm finding fewer grand mansions and gated communities than I'd expected. No doubt the gorgeous houses are tucked away in what one writer called "the coombe-furrowed Chilterns", but on my beaten track, life is reassuringly normal.

I cycle on, passing the famous BT Tower – a real inland lighthouse – overlooking the M40. Then, before I know it, I leave Bucks for Oxfordshire, speeding down Aston Hill. Somewhere in the hollow to my right, a tenth-century battle raged between the locals and the ever-marauding Danes. There are juniper trees down there too. Juniper, according to an excellent local legend, only prospers where human blood has been spilt. That's exactly the kind of folk memory that I can normally savour for a good 5 miles on a long ride, but at this precise moment I'm screaming downhill, concentrating on staying upright. The gradient, the curves and some persistent traffic mean it's a case of fingers clenched tight on the brakes, eyes peeled for the slightest pothole. The fastest cyclist on the Strava app took this stretch at 63.3 km/hour, I later discover. Funnily enough you won't find me in any top tens.

After Aston Hill, I decide to divert to Aston Rowant – as ever on the hunt for an older version of my road. This village is more prosperous, but I ignore the well-thatched cottages and precisely clipped hedges to bump my way down a rutted track past the church. The route – a continuation of the Piddington holloway – was known as "The London Weye" in medieval times. Here it crosses the Lower Icknield Way – an even more ancient thoroughfare used by drovers with their sheep and cattle. For those without a soul, this so-called Five Ways is a scruffy intersection of Chiltern footpaths. For the rest of us, it's an ancient meeting place, once trodden by the Tudor Princess Elizabeth as she made her way to Woodstock – and house arrest – during the reign of Queen Mary. I'm so impressed that I decide on a longer diversion, getting off the bike to walk the diagonal path towards the next village – effectively the fifth of the five ways. According to the shiny new interpretation board back at the junction, the remains of a "pest house" lie beneath this field of yet-to-ripen wheat. Presumably it was a place of exile during times of plague. Heaven knows what an archaeological dig would reveal all these centuries later.

After lifting the bike over a number of stiles – God's way of punishing cyclists who stray onto footpaths – I arrive in Postcombe, another "blink and you'll miss it" village. But cycling conditions are now excellent – and quite often downhill. This may be the main A40 but the vast majority of the traffic has been syphoned off onto the M40. Having said that, the noise from the motorway is becoming more of a persistent nuisance than a background thrum, increasing as I climb into Tetsworth – as green as Stokenchurch and with more character. In Edwardian times the major inn was The Swan – which must have put on a good show when Harper came calling:

The imaginative man, who stays, to his great delight at the comfortable old 'Swan' can repeople it with the bustle and circumstance of road-faring any time during the last two centuries; can see the dignified heads of the University come... and can witness again the eloping couples, eager to change horses and be off.

The Swan is now an auction house but remains rambling and charismatic, chock-a-block full of ancient furniture, ornaments and books. I happen to arrive in the middle of a more modern kind of bustle: TV crews are filming the antiques expert Paul Martin, who is gesticulating precisely and authoritatively – clearly in full "piece to camera" mode.

I get all of the gossip down the road at The Red Lion.

"We're normally *Midsomer Murders* round here," says the lady behind the bar.

"I don't know what this one is all about."

"We do. We're doing the transport," pipes up one of two lads enjoying cheesy chips at the window.

"It's called *The Great Auction Showdown*. They're doing all the background filming today. The auction bit is tomorrow."

We are then all distracted by two red kites directly outside. A successful reintroduction programme for these huge birds of prey started in the Chilterns in 1989 – and they still seem to love the A40 corridor. I feel as if they have been providing me with close air support ever since I crossed into Oxfordshire. Here, they are excelling themselves. Repeated low passes, plying and playing the thermals. They also seem to be dive-bombing an innocent blackbird just for the hell of it – a cruel avian airshow laid on specially for us.

"We're from Milton Keynes," says the younger of the two drivers, seemingly awestruck.

"We don't get this round our way."

_____

Given wings by a Red Lion coffee, I fly west. For once I seem to be on schedule. I'm certainly enjoying myself, eating up the first 20 miles of the day with ease. At Milton Common I notice that the former Three Pigeons pub has followed The Swan into the antiques trade. Here the key phrase is "architectural salvage". It's up-market of course. Leafing through a catalogue, I find an English verd antique and rose siena marble doorcase in the Beaux Arts style. Yours for around £15,000.

I start to feel the gravitational pull of Oxford on the outskirts of Wheatley. Here the A40 gets mixed up with the motorway and it gets uncomfortable for cyclists. But the village beyond is charming – red brick replaced by creamy limestone for the first time. Harper got his sketch pad out here. In fastidious pen and ink, he records a hunched figure with an umbrella walking along Church Road, ignoring what would appear to be a church steeple on the side of the road – at ground level. It's actually an unusually shaped lock-up – a place where ne'er-do-wells could be incarcerated overnight. Happily, it survives to this day. According to Harper:

Quite sixty years have passed since a prisoner was thrust into its window-less, unventilated keeping, and it now serves the combined useful offices of a storehouse for gardening tools and the home of the village stocks, which, like itself, have long outlived their usefulness.

But was it ever used for its intended purpose? Local historians can find no evidence that the agricultural rioters it was aimed at ever languished here. They are equally insistent that it was never used for mere drunkards – though of course that's the urban myth.

I faff around with the phone camera, trying to find Harper's precise spot. Lock-ups are relatively common in villages. But this appears to be the only one built as a tall, hexagonal pyramid. Its shape doesn't make my composition any easier, but close comparison between the photo and his sketch reveals that in the 120 years between our visits very little has changed.

Road-wise, there are several variations along a London to Oxford theme. The modern A40 of course, the London Road with its generous verges and the more shaded Old London Road. In fairness the A40 has got the right idea. Beyond Wheatley, it skirts northwards to avoid the 560-foot-high Shotover Hill. But my mantra on these rides is to take the original route wherever possible. Sometimes they can prove tricky to find, but a street called "Old Road" in the suburb of Littleworth removes any doubt.

I should rejoice that it's so easy; I actually feel cheated out of a challenge.

It's immediately clear why the horses hated it. Old Road is a slog, with only an impressively sweeping view north towards the Vale of Aylesbury in compensation. The tarmac then deteriorates into a rough track of lumpy earth and stone. It's dry for me, but a quote from Harper made clear his frustration in these parts. What on earth do they make the roads with in Oxfordshire, he asked:

> Not honest macadam, but the local limestone, which becomes buttery when rained upon... The Recording Angel does not book the curses expended by cyclists and drivers of motor-cars upon the road-makers and road-surface in Oxfordshire, because he understands the dire provocation coming from the attempts made to perform the almost impossible feats of keeping upright or out of the ditches when these perilous ways are muddy.

Edwardian gent Charles George Harper, effing and jeffing? Surely not.

For some reason I was expecting a forest at the top, instead I cross a broad greensward set between trees, though these hedges are plenty thick enough to provide cover for highwaymen. I try to imagine how vulnerable early stagecoach passengers must have felt, but somehow my imagination can't get past the kitsch "Stand and Deliver" video by Adam and the

Ants – such is the power of early 1980s editions of *Top of the Pops* for those of us of a certain age.

I get off the bike and lean it against an oak. Putting the earphones in, I skip forward a couple of decades and listen to "Shotover Hill" by Supergrass. The Oxfordshire-based band are better known for urgent indie pop, but I prefer their slower, Beatles-inspired psychedelia. Certainly it all seems to make sense in this buttercup-filled meadow. Much as in Bottom Wood, I disappear into my own world, this time soaking up local lyrics. It's such a luxury to be running to my own timetable, without a schedule, without a care, beholden to no one. In fact my only disappointment is that the leafiness of the tree canopy means I never quite get to look down on the "dreaming spires" which presumably lie directly below.

Eventually I pull myself together and return to the bike which, I now realize, is in a right state. The wheat field has left a sheen of green dust across every surface. What's more, a residue of Postcombe sheep excrement disfigures the tyres. I'm hardly ready for the bright lights of Oxford, but a clean-up will have to wait as I enjoy another steep descent off Shotover's western slopes, shooting over an eastern bypass and into its comfortable suburbs.

I know that I'm in Oxford because both pedestrians and drivers are respectful of cyclists – on and off the cycle paths. What's more, I seem to be the only one wearing a helmet. In this city, riders have long since reached that critical mass where you don't wear special stuff to get on a bike, you just get on a bike. Final confirmation comes when I pass a bloke carrying a tyre-less back wheel through the streets, complete with rear cassette. Rare in Uxbridge, I would argue. Gloriously unremarkable in Oxford.

My downhill run continues too – today has been a complete doddle effort-wise. I eventually hit rush-hour traffic at St Clements. But we cyclists easily weave our way through the cars so that I cross the River Cherwell via Magdalen Bridge full of early evening optimism. From that very first glance of Magdalen Tower, it's clear this place is special. Magdalen College can boast of alumni as varied as poet laureate John Betjeman, King Edward VIII, the dramatist Oscar Wilde and the businesswoman Martha Lane Fox. But here, that sort of list isn't at all extraordinary. In fact it may even be considered lightweight. For example, they haven't had a prime minister – though ten other colleges have. In fact this city claims an impressive 28 PMs in total, including – most recently – Rishi Sunak, Liz Truss, Boris Johnson, Theresa May and David Cameron.

I have now been thrust very much into "gown" rather than "town"; the part of the city known for what Harper called "its collegiate gravity". As a result, I get off the bike to enjoy the spectacularly beautiful buildings lining both sides of the high street at a slower pace. Intriguing chinks of lime green quadrangle can be glimpsed beyond ancient porters' lodges, but it's not immediately obvious what's what. Colleges don't do anything as vulgar as signs; they've been here far too long for that. In fact I have to smile when it's the bus stop outside Brasenose that announces that fact to me rather than the building itself.

The street they call "The High" bends slowly westward, with a sycamore tree at the halfway point, apparently the only landmark to be visible from both ends. The architectural author Nikolaus Pevsner declared that the slight curve helps make it "one of the world's great streets". Quite a claim.

After some lonely miles, a period of people-watching is called for. My preferred place for this is Jericho Coffee Traders, a scruffy café two-thirds of the way down The High. Somehow the uncomfortable benches on the pavement add to the charm – especially when two Aussie tourists are up for a chat. They're following the Thames from source to sea on foot. But, like me, they're taking in the sights.

"No point rushing," says the older of the two.

"We're only doing about twelve ks a day. Start at half nine, all done by three."

Then with a sweep of the hand: "That way we get to have a decent look around."

Hear, hear.

At that moment, another gaggle of students walks past, wearing formal gowns and carrying garlands of flowers. The Aussies ask me what the fuss is about – turning to the native as an expert – but I shrug my shoulders. I suggest they might be choristers – perhaps because I am looking for an evensong service to attend a little later. But that doesn't seem quite right. There's some sort of hushed excitement about the place that we can't explain.

In any case I need to visit Carfax Tower before it closes. If Oxford has a dead centre, it's Carfax – all that remains of a medieval church at The High's eastern end. Indeed, this being Oxford, the word Carfax is derived from the Latin word for four roads coming together – *quadrifurcus*. You don't get that sort of reference so much in Hayes End or High Wycombe. As well as giving me a firm geographical bearing, the tower offers the chance of a bird's eye view for just £3. So I lock the bike up at its base and climb its 99 stairs. The panorama is all the more impressive for not being *too* high. Oxford is a compact city, I realize, ringed by the green trees of the Chilterns on one side and the smoother contours of the Cotswolds on the other. Cornmarket Street to the north and Queen Street to the west are pedestrianized, so a steady stream of open-top buses wheel round from St Aldate's, their passengers looking down on those below, perhaps unaware that some of us are spying on them too.

Back at the coffee house I'd decided that Merton College was the place for evensong. And in trying to find its chapel, I stumble across The Examination Schools – and the answer to the Aussies' question. So this, I realize, is what the fuss is about. A giant marquee constructed on the lawn outside and a street packed with people. Relieved-looking students emerge from the building to be congratulated by friends offering bouquets.

"What's happening?" I shout, struggling to be heard above a happy hubbub.

"We've just finished our exams!" responds one man with a modest whoop and a clenched fist.

"So tonight's a big night out in Oxford then?"

"Well it is if you're a chemist."

Ah, just those studying chemistry. Presumably Oxford looks like this every June evening as the academic year comes to its climax, subject by subject.

I find the entrance to Merton College on a cobbled back street and present myself at The Porters' Lodge. There is nowhere obvious to store my bike, but an elegant solution is found and I won't embarrass the helpful people who made it happen. The Australians have arrived too – on my recommendation, it appears. Collectively out of our depth with procedure and etiquette, we are permitted to make our way through the grounds to the chapel where an organist in a flowing purple cassock is engaged in last-minute rehearsals – his declaratory musical statements given all the more force by larger than life mannerisms.

The more unshaven of the two Aussies leans across to me with a stage whisper.

"It's not exactly Pink Floyd, is it, mate?"

We chuckle mischievously, like teenagers at the back of the school bus. And then file into our pews, reverence restored. The chapel looks majestic – a massive east window, fantastic detail in the wooden roof and original stained glass. Worship has been offered here since the thirteenth century; this kind of service since the seventeenth.

I'm far from an evensong regular, but in my humble opinion the sound is like nothing else on earth. Here, 30 choristers face each other across the chapel, their voices producing a remarkable amalgam. I am particularly affected by *Libera nos*: a "petition to the Holy Trinity for freedom, redemption and absolution" written approximately 500 years ago by Magdalen College's John Sheppard. His composition creates wave after wave of harmony; somehow both ancient and modern; somehow both haunting and soothing.

It comes to a close, the choirmaster's horizontal hand signals indicating a musical full stop. But then there's an other-worldly pause as the acoustics of the chapel allow the choristers' last bars a second life, swirling upward, untethered from those lungs below. I'm one of about 35 in the congregation, all seemingly mesmerized, some closing their eyes as if to soak it up more completely.

I'm Catholic by upbringing. I understand "church". I am not mystified or discombobulated by the ritual as such. But I didn't grow up with evensong. And Anglican evensong from the Book of Common Prayer is a different world. As I walk out of the chapel some 45 minutes later to the most fearsome of organ voluntaries from our man in purple, I feel as if I have been plugged into a higher voltage. How you square that with my agnosticism I just don't know.

I return to Carfax Tower – as much to re-orientate myself as anything else – and head west. In this direction, Oxford declines from "world-class city centre" to "any old outskirts" remarkably quickly. But newer parts of the university find a home amid a shopping mall and multi-storey car parks. Nuffield College was founded by the car manufacturer William Morris; the Said Business School in honour of the Syrian–Saudi–Canadian businessman Wafic Said. These twentieth-century buildings will feel hallowed in time, I'm sure.

Once again I am travelling at a decent pace, but I finally concede to myself that I am being helped by a decent following wind. Most of us cyclists do this, don't we? Conduct an internal commentary on our own performance as though viewed from a helicopter above. Part pep talk, part Cognitive Behavioural Therapy. Truth be told, my easterly has probably been with me ever since St Paul's Cathedral. But until now it's suited me to think it's all the result of a newly improved, peak condition kind of me. The truth is that I'm getting a helping hand from the cycling gods – and long may that continue. The bike is behaving itself too. Smooth, free-running and puncture-free as I bowl along. But let's not jinx it.

———

For a county that I consider to be bumpy, the terrain to the west of Oxford is surprisingly flat. And as a result, it's watery. The casual observer might just see that familiar "edge of" landscape – car showrooms, supermarkets and DIY warehouses – but a look at the wider map shows reservoirs, lakes, brooks and streams. In the suburb of Botley, I seem to be continually crossing waterways – indeed Harper called this street Seven Bridges Road.

Next, I turn right onto the Eynsham Road, soon leaving the houses – and the cycle lanes – behind. It's never really got warm but the sky is blue and the setting serene for the final few miles of my day. Every so often I see a bike at the roadside – normally chained to something or other and covered in brightly coloured crocheted wool. It takes me a while to work out they are the visual symbols of a local campaign for a cycle path along this very stretch. People commute from these villages into Oxford, runs the argument, let them cycle there in safety. Difficult to argue with, I'd have thought. Extrapolating further – as I always do when my brain is set in bike mode – all it needs is a network of successful local schemes to make longer treks like my own a lot safer and more popular.

I'm now approaching the Thames. In the old days it held the whip hand around here – its marshy floodplains making travel difficult. Taming this landscape took time and money. A distinguished Oxford lawyer called Sir William Blackstone made it his retirement project in the 1760s, knocking heads together to improve the Seven Bridges causeway and replace an unreliable ferry at Swinford with a toll bridge.

But, as is often the way, it was the local landowner who ultimately benefited. Willoughby Bertie, Fourth Earl of Abingdon, was a carefree nob with a reputation for frivolity and poor business acumen. But the only way that Sir William could get the finances to work was by getting the tolls to be paid to the earl's family in perpetuity. Bertie was involved in building an inn alongside the bridge. Everything went wrong with that – and it has not survived. Everything went right with Blackstone's bridge, which still looks great more than 250 years later.

Swinford Bridge remains one of the wonders of this way to Wales – and it is still a toll bridge. For obscure reasons that I prefer not to understand, the tariff is ludicrously cheap. Every car pays just five pence to cross; for single-decker buses it's a relatively extortionate 12 pence while longer lorries are charged at "10 pence per axle". But it can mean queues – even if cyclists get waved through.

The knock-on effects of this one piece of civil engineering were far-reaching. Travellers heading to Gloucester and Wales were no longer pushed south via Faringdon. Instead they could head to Witney and beyond without as much as a damp boot. Many a nineteenth-century Cotswold innkeeper had cause to raise a tankard to the first Vinerian Professor of English Law even if they hadn't heard of him.

Fun fact: Sir William still gets quoted in US Supreme Court judgments.

Tonight I'm too late for the toll collectors so I have all the time in the world to take in the scene. This young Thames is already looking like a decent river. The bridge – three bays of ashlar limestone with elegant balustraded parapets – frames it nicely. But it's the tollhouse that really takes my fancy. Small semi-circular windows on the ground floor look out across the river; large first-floor panes keep a watchful eye on the road. Travellers can't fail to notice the single word "TOLL" painted in black capitals on a bright white background. Perfectly legible. Admirably succinct.

Its very survival cheers me immensely. It's a sign that I'm escaping the London bubble. Surely such time-wasting idiosyncrasies wouldn't be tolerated closer to the capital?

Neighbouring Eynsham has a similar feel – a charming market square and a scattering of ancient-looking pubs. It also contains my bed for the night. Yesterday it was a Travelodge, tonight it's an Airbnb. I have to admit that despite (or because of?) the slightly forced cheeriness, I never quite feel at home in someone else's house. But the bike is safe, the rent reasonable, and the room more than satisfactory for my needs.

I check my stats and I check the forecast. Today is set to be by far the easiest of my eight on the road. Tomorrow will be hotter, tomorrow will be longer and tomorrow will be steeper.

DAY THREE

EYNSHAM TO GLOUCESTER

Day Three

Eynsham to
Gloucester

51 miles
3,438 ft of ascent

GLOUCESTER

Seven Springs

Northleach

Burford

EYNSHAM

Birdlip

Witney

N

NW

NE

W

E

SW

SE

S

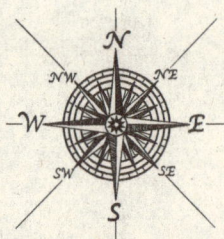

Direction of travel

EYNSHAM TO
GLOUCESTER

It's bin day in Eynsham. And a number of residents like nothing better than to wheel them out noisily and early – from 5.30 a.m. in fact. I can't face the bright screen of a phone, so I reach for something more analogue – a map of the Cotswolds. I've yet to reach its eastern edge, but I'm hoping that it will see me through from my first coffee to mid-afternoon.

I bought OL45 about two years ago and it's already well-used, admittedly more as a source of relaxation rather than on location. Doesn't everyone unwind on the sofa with Ordnance Survey after work? OK, it's just me pleading guilty to tracing the river valleys, weighing alternative routes and enjoying the variety of odd names that every sheet brings. Here, almost without trying, I can find Guggle Wood near Taynton; the hamlet of Ready Token and the single word "Poverty" mysteriously sited close to an unremarkable B-road south of Little Barrington.

What should we call this? Armchair travel? Contour contemplation? Cartographical day-dreaming on a Cotswold theme? Take your pick. I've always seen it as a down payment on a future adventure, whatever my wife's look of bemusement has suggested back home.

By 6.30 a.m. I realize that sleep ain't happening, so I draw the curtains and take stock of my surroundings. This very house is made of some sort of limestone, perhaps not as fine as that chosen for Oxford colleges, but warm, attractive and no doubt hewn locally. As the refuse lorry klaxon bleats in a nearby cul-de-sac I return to the map, in particular the landscape close to the wriggling River Windrush. Tucked in around the copses and the plantations one feature comes up again and again: "Quarry (dis)". Within the double fold that sits naturally in my hand, I quickly count 20 disused quarries in all. To this cyclist, the Oxford links, the quality of the stone and the lie of the land are diversions just waiting to happen. Not ideal when there are 50 *direct* miles to be negotiated, but probably irresistible nevertheless.

It's not a day to hang about. So by 8 a.m. I have politely negotiated the do-si-do around my hosts for the use of the family bathroom and gulped down a breakfast. I then repack so that I can be outside the Mill Street Post Office as it opens. One more parcel plus £3.49 equals an even slimmer pannier.

Back on the A40, I duck and dive on the road's fringes, taking an old course via the hamlet of Barnard Gate for example, rather than the bypass. To my surprise this extended lay-by contains a pub as well as a smattering of houses. Sadly The Boot Inn lies boarded up, save for the sliver of a functioning post box within the front wall. Perhaps the newer road removed the trade as well as traffic. Known for many a decade as The Britannia, it was renamed in the 1990s to match a growing display of shoes collected from famous people like Stanley Matthews, Simon Le Bon and George Best. The word is that a bottle of Dom Pérignon donated by a charismatic landlord worked wonders in persuading the celebrity to walk away in their socks. But today's closely nailed plywood means there's no chance of seeing as much as a David Gower loafer.

Instead, I head round to the back, where a black poplar has fallen square across what I suspect was the kitchen block. It has reacted philosophically; re-sprouting at regular intervals along a now horizontal trunk. And proof that it's still alive comes with the aroma – a gentle scent of balsam hanging in the air above the beer garden. Will that smell ever compete with stale lager and cheese and onion crisps? You'd have to doubt it.

I look out at the fields beyond. In my neck of the woods, marsh harriers and buzzards are the dominant birds of prey. Here, once again, it's red kites – four, splitting the sky between them. For the first time I identify their cry – I have such a grandstand view I can hardly fail to. It's a squeaking mew, perhaps less plaintive and certainly more repetitive than a buzzard's.

From there, I go up what I think is Cogges Hill but come down something the signposts call Oxford Hill. Either way, as I approach Witney I'm pretty sure I'm on the same road that Harper would have taken all those years ago. A bridge over the Windrush now lies between me and the town centre. I decide to sit on its squat parapet, reach for his Volume One and try to get my head around the product for which this town was famous. In a word: blankets.

My Edwardian companion is, as ever, a master of *place*.

What would Witney be without that famous stream? Why, just a little agricultural village. You come over it by a stone bridge on entering the town, and see it foaming past the old mills and blanket factories, from its 18 miles' course up in the north of Gloucestershire; and thinking of it... become presently lost in thoughts upon the old English manufactories when industries depended upon natural geographical advantages, before science came to put its heavy foot in the scale and upset the balance.

Beautifully done, sir.

Those geographical advantages were rolling fields just perfect for sheep, a river powerful enough to help with the heavy work of turning wool into cloth and – like High Wycombe – proximity to the prosperous markets of London and the south east.

As a result, Witney survived as a centre for blanket-making until well after Harper's time, only withering in the face of two more recent arrivals – central heating and the duvet. The timing, now I think about it, exactly mirrors my childhood. We moved to our first house with radiators in the early 1970s. Duvets followed a few years later. By the mid 1980s even your grandma had relegated blankets to a cupboard, only to be used in case of a very cold winter. Witney's staple product had gone from being solidly dependable to irredeemably naff in little more than a generation.

I can see the results of that decline from this very spot. On the east bank of the Windrush, the vast Bridge Street mill once produced almost half a million blankets a year. It's now a mixture of old buildings put to new uses and modern flats. A short cycle down nearby Mill Street opens up a view of a tall chimney once used to help power the Early's factory – the last of the companies to fold.

I return to the bridge and start walking towards the town centre, but within yards a sandwich board points the way to Witney Blanket Hall:

Free Admittance
Please Come in
Woollen Blankets and Throws
Coffee, Pies and Assemblies since 1721.

Coffee, pies and assemblies? They're pretty much my three favourite things. How can I resist?

Witney Blanket Hall was built by the Company of Witney Blanket Weavers as a place to both show off their wares and enforce their standards. The assistant is quickly over to welcome me. This is the Measuring Room, she tells me, where the size and quality of every blanket in the district was recorded. Upstairs is the Great Room where business deals were thrashed out. Today the shelves are stacked with what look like blankets for sale, except of course that no one needs such things any more. They're actually "throws" – a fantastic bit of rebranding. A 60" by 76" Shetland Chevron design will set you back £96. I wonder what those bigwigs would make of the fact that while blankets are almost banned from the bedroom, they now seem obligatory in our living rooms, draped over sofas.

In the Great Room, up-tempo classical music breezes out from hidden speakers. On display there's everything from wooden loom shuttles to grey blankets woven for a nuclear shelter. "Good to know that Witney blankets were once recognized as a legitimate defence against such an attack," deadpans the official leaflet.

Elsewhere there's a photo explaining the industry's accidental contribution to the language. It shows dozens of blankets being hung out on wooden frames to bleach and dry. The frames were called tenters, with the accompanying pegs known as tenterhooks: a hardy English metaphor with its origins firmly attached to fields on the banks of the Windrush.

To the rear, a narrow yard runs down to the river. You can't really call it a garden because the space is split between outhouses, café tables and a more formal courtyard. It is instead a burgage plot – the classic medieval arrangement for a market town. Access to the main street was critical and precious. Each property owner – or burgess – only got a slim frontage. But behind, every square foot was worked. Metal might be hammered in workshops, livestock reared and slaughtered, vegetables sown and harvested. Here, they brewed beer too. Walking up and down is like turning back time.

I re-emerge onto the high street and take another look at the building. I'm struggling for a description, but luckily the architectural experts agreed that this is "provincial Baroque" – two words that I'm not sure I have ever seen side by side before. The clock face is worth a second glance too. They've made a conscious decision to give it just the one hand – an hour hand.

Initially I'm in denial that this could have ever been a thing. But a quick Google suggests that it was actually the norm until the second half of the eighteenth century – in other words minute hands were once a crazy modern affectation. Pondering further, I come to terms with the fact that people once lived with a much looser interpretation of time. And finally I decide to take it as an instruction for the rest of my ride. After all, whenever I travel by bike there's an element of "I'll be there around…" rather than "I'll see you at…". To some extent that's down to the vagaries of cycling, but it's probably as much to do with my attitude.

I wander more, perhaps I wonder more too. I chat quite a bit, I relax rather a lot. Yes, the GPS on the Strava app is ticking over in the background, but I like to think that as far as the rhythm of the day is concerned, there is only one hand on my internal clock.

Either way, from now on, I'm running on blanket time.

———

Witney gets more prosperous as you head west. The high street soon becomes the tree-lined Market Green, with the heart of the town clearly marked by the Butter Cross facing the Town Hall. It's one of those covered market buildings simultaneously adored and ignored by locals. Adored on grounds of civic pride; ignored because no one really needs to sell fresh butter from within a forest of thick stone pillars any more. The eighteenth-century Town Hall is grander – two storeys, the first-floor meeting room above a colonnaded ground floor open to the elements. Their style and their proximity to each other provide another reminder of High Wycombe, although Home Counties red brick has now been upgraded to Cotswold stone. Beyond them lies the beautiful Church Green – St Mary's sitting at one end of what almost feels like a cathedral close overlooked by pollarded lime trees.

I head out of town via Corn Street, negotiate a roundabout and weave through a housing estate where my request for directions from a chap working underneath a car gets answered in an Oxfordshire burr – the first I've heard. I am then painfully slow to realize that today's B4047 must have been the original highway heading west. Funnily enough, the most obvious way from A to B is often the oldest too.

But within a mile I can't resist a slight detour, dropping steeply into the valley of the Windrush towards the village of Minster Lovell. It's one of those gorgeous descents that draw you in suddenly, even as you realize that what goes down must come up. I'm not the only one. This appears to be a favourite route for families – as witnessed by a variety of brightly coloured bikes and some slightly erratic steering methods. Yep, start them young.

At the bottom of the hill, the stone bridge slowly reveals itself to be more of a causeway. Clearly today's pussycat of a river has angrier moods. Rosebay willowherb sways in a light breeze. A red admiral and a peacock butterfly hunt for nectar beneath me, while on the far bank a flutter of small whites dance across the meadow. The Windrush is quickly establishing itself as an entrancing river and I happily "waste" peaceful moments just taking in the scene. Blanket time, indeed.

Minster Lovell's main street lies just beyond the scenic Wash Meadow cricket ground. The houses nearby are similarly cute. In particular, the competition for best-kept thatched looks stiff. (If push came to shove, I'd give it to Tullochs Cottage halfway down on the left.) But I'm here for the ruins of Minster Lovell Hall – not least because

Harper describes them as being "one of the most romantic places, both in the beauty of its site and in the incidents of its story". To my surprise they lie unheralded and un-signposted behind St Kenelm's Church. Only a succession of cars parked close against the hedgerow gives the game away. Visitors must walk past the church and its many headstones, then through a graveyard extension. A young boy, seeing the latter, turns to his mum, arms akimbo and asks "more dead bodies?" in mock despair.

If only he knew the full story. This place had belonged to the aristocratic Lovell family since the early twelfth century. I'm here to pay my respects to Francis Lovell who changed sides during the Wars of the Roses approximately 300 years later. First a Lancastrian, then a Yorkist, he was last seen fleeing the site of the Battle of Stoke – the Yorkists' last attempt to unseat Henry VII. Some say that Lovell fled abroad. But according to Oxfordshire legend he returned to the family seat. Regarded as a traitor by the new regime, he hoped to live out his life alone in an underground room – his needs met by one servant sworn to secrecy.

Fast forward another couple of centuries to 1708 when workmen accidentally broke into a vault, to be greeted by the sight of a man's skeleton seated at a table with an open book, paper and pen beside him. Harper wrote, gleefully:

Whether the servant yielded to treachery, or was killed or died, will never be known, the fact remains that the

unfortunate Lord Lovell, having exhausted his stock of
food, was starved to death in his secret hiding place.

English Heritage is quite good at making sites like this free
and open during – as the sign puts it – "any reasonable
daylight hours". And today the usual kind of people are
tramping around in decent numbers: elderly couples, dog
walkers, lone ramblers; all reading the information boards
quietly and diligently. There's the odd picnic rug too and
one family's kids boisterously switch between balancing on
walls and splashing in the river beyond. From high above the
parapets of the south west tower, I notice that the gargoyles
are grimacing down upon all of us. Benevolently I think.

I retrace my steps to Wash Meadow and climb steeply back
towards the old road on the approach to Worsham. Harper
tells a good story of how single horsemen felt haunted along
this stretch. They would turn up in either Witney or Burford
to tell of a "little man, dressed in black" who would suddenly
emerge from the undergrowth, trying to grab their reins.

Harper pooh-poohs such claims before adding:

But stay! – what was it that gave the present writer that
bad side-slip he experienced here returning to Witney
[by bike] on the black night of a wet day?

I sail through Worsham Bottom without incident and turn
right just before the old road rejoins the new. Another half

a mile should see me reach my next village, but the road goes on and on until I reach a T-junction which simply shouldn't be there. I consult the map to realize that I've taken a wrong turn and ridden needless miles. Only later do I accept that I've clearly become the latest victim of "Old Black Stockings", though I can't say I saw the pesky little'un myself.

In any case it's not the worst time to go wrong. The sun is out and the hedgerows are alive with birdsong. As the temperature rises towards 20 degrees, the jacket gets stowed in the pannier for the first time – another good reason for that trip to the post office. Even better, the only way to get me back on track involves a downhill ride to Asthall and the first of several churchyards to completely beguile me.

Set on a sloping site, St Nicholas' looks picture-perfect. Here, I see my first "bale tomb" – a distinctive style of sarcophagus unique to the Cotswolds, in fact pretty much unique to the Windrush valley. They're difficult to describe – between 2 and 3 feet high, elaborately decorated and barrel-topped. Here, it's as though a pirate's wooden treasure chest has been left out in the sun so long it's turned to stone. Legend has it that their size was also handy when it came to hiding venison poached from the nearby Wychwood Forest.

Parked at the roadside, I am surprised to find a London cab, a fact I mention to the chap mooching about nearby.

"I know. It's mine," he beams, in an accent more East End than West Oxon.

It turns out he's ferrying an American couple and their guide on a personalized *Downton Abbey* tour of Olde England. The *Downton* bit involves the village of Bampton – some 5 miles south of the A40 – where much of the filming took place. This stop is to see Asthall Manor House, looking down on the churchyard and famous as the home of the six aristocratic Mitford sisters who came to prominence during the 1930s. Nancy Mitford is probably the most well-known – she wrote *Love in a Cold Climate* – a satire of the British upper classes published in 1949. But as a set of siblings they are quite remarkable. *The Times* journalist Ben Macintyre famously summarized them as "Diana the Fascist, Jessica the Communist, Unity the Hitler-lover, Nancy the novelist, Deborah the Duchess and Pamela the unobtrusive poultry connoisseur". You really couldn't have made them up.

But why are the Americans here in the first place?

"We LOVE *Downton*," says Geoff from North Carolina.

"*Downton* got us through Covid, it really did. And we promised ourselves that once it was all over we would come and see it for ourselves."

I can't argue with a word of that, in fact I even succumb to a moment of gentle patriotic pride. The church is listed. The Manor House is listed. Even my bale tomb to the memory of the Fletcher Family is Grade II. Swallows are swooping in and out of a tiny crevice in the church's north door and the temperature has stealthily crept up from "pleasant" to "balmy".

The guide politely looks at his watch and nods to the driver. A pub lunch awaits and he's on a schedule. But the Americans want to drink in the scene one last time. I'm with them. In fact I'm happy just *watching* them appreciating the scene. The London cab, the peaceful churchyard, the historical family home. Are any of us going to find anything quite as English as this during the remainder of our journeys?

—————

I barrel along more narrow lanes towards Swinbrook and a pub that might just be about to welcome the Americans. Certainly it has both *Downton* and Mitford connections. The sisters moved to Swinbrook when they were slightly older and The Swan remembers them with photos on the wall. I'm not sure where else in the country a known Nazi and confirmed Fascist would be quite so "venerated", but I guess I understand the historical point. Meanwhile diehard *Downton* fans will know that The Swan was the place where Lady Sybil and Branson stayed en route to Gretna Green for an attempted elopement.

And from there it's not far to the town of Burford. I meet the main street halfway down a steep hill, lined with the most honey-coloured of limestone buildings. The houses feel timeless, with upstairs windows often half-dormered within the roofs for added charm.

The church lies further down the hill. St John the Baptist is set in a sheltered spot sloping towards a mill stream fed by the Windrush. Once inside, I buy the church history booklet. Of course I do. I've read dozens over the years, enough to feel as though I'm almost a connoisseur of these labours of love. Burford's is glossy, well-presented and beautifully written. It's also the most exciting I have ever encountered. Exciting? Well, it includes details on the Tanfields, grasping aristocratic landlords who were so hated by their tenants that they were burned in effigy for more than 200 years; a seventeenth-century killing where the murderer got off by bribing the jury; an eighteenth-century vicar described as "a common drunkard" who terrorized his wife, seduced his maid and lived "at a barber's in a mean manner" rather than at the vicarage; and a nineteenth-century Whit Sunday feast so wild that, nine months later, "a number of illegitimate births were annually expected".

Lest that should all be too racy, its 32 pages are also excellent on sixteenth-century heretics, a tomb from the same era illustrated with members of an Amazonian tribe ("the earliest representation in Britain of inhabitants of the New World") and a nineteenth-century church restoration so drastic that it prompted the Arts and Crafts designer William Morris to form the Society for the Protection of Ancient Buildings after a stand-up row with Burford's vicar who told him "the church, sir, is mine and if I choose to, I shall stand on my head in it".

And I've yet to even mention the most infamous incident to take place within this holy ground. It happened during the English Civil War. In the months after King Charles I lost his head, hundreds of soldiers mutinied, fed up with a lack of pay and the prospect of being sent to Ireland. Among them were many so-called Levellers – people with the sort of radical views that even Oliver Cromwell blanched at. More than 1,000 were in the process of marching from Salisbury to Banbury when they were ambushed by Parliamentarian forces overnight in Burford. Hundreds escaped, but 340 others were captured and imprisoned within the church. Three days later, after a court martial, the ringleaders were shot in the churchyard on Cromwell's orders. The remainder were made to watch the ordeal from the church roof.

For centuries their deaths remained an unheralded postscript to a turbulent time. But since 1975 all that has changed. Now Cornet Thompson, Corporal Perkins and Private Church are seen as pioneers, campaigning for freedom of the press, freedom of religion and regular parliaments; dangerously radical to their contemporaries, worthy of our admiration today.

So the last time I stood in this churchyard it looked very different. I made a special trip for the first annual Levellers Day ceremony since Covid. It started rather unpromisingly with perhaps just 20 or 30 people loitering around. True, they didn't look like National Trust types and I guess you don't often see takeaway coffee cups temporarily balanced on bale tombs. But then the sound of voices filled the air and a choir of a dozen women took centre stage; the Sea Green Singers, decked in turquoise and specializing in songs of the radical left. These secular hymns acted as a rallying cry and soon many more gathered, flags fluttering: the North Oxfordshire Socialist Alliance, the Oxford Labour Party and Extinction Rebellion. Only then did I notice a beautifully detailed banner leaning against the church titled "Levellers Day Burford 1649", together with a key quote from the time:

For Really I think that the poorest he, that is in England
Have a Life to live as the greatest he.

(Try it again with "man" replacing "he" and you get the idea. Any sense of female equality was still a long way off.)

As the bells rang out for 11 a.m., the minister called us to order. Carefully acknowledging that he had a congregation of all faiths and none, he put the Levellers in their historical context; they were among the first to argue for what we would now call human rights and they'd died bravely in their pursuit. A minute's silence was imperfectly observed by the jackdaws nesting above the south door, but earnestly so by the rest of us. A meditation on a different England, an England at war with itself, an England where the king had been beheaded, but where those in power were now anxious to put the brakes on a torrent of new ideas.

Later, about 200 people had marched in unison from Church Green round to the high street. We were led by the inimitable punk poet Attila the Stockbroker, singing songs from his Civil War album (*Restoration Tragedy*) and somehow flitting between recorder and fiddle – a remarkable performance.

Today, as I walk my bike along the same route, I find Burford to be resolutely quiet with hints of small "c" conservatism. But never forget, once a year they belt out "The Internationale" here; the Sea Green Singers singing the verses so sweetly, the gnarled old Reds growling out the chorus, fists held defiantly aloft.

I need coffee. And I choose The Priory café on the high street because on previous visits, they've always been happy to allow me to manhandle the bike through the shop, down the steps and into the garden. It's another classic burgage plot, repurposed with tables, chairs and parasols, so perhaps this is just ancient, burgess etiquette. Over the obligatory flat white and cake, I take another look at the church booklet. It turns out I've missed important stuff. So, after refuelling, I return to St John's for a final sweep. On the top of the font, I pick out the lead bearing the misspelt graffiti of one of the Levellers: "Anthony Sedley 1649 Prisner". What a survivor that is. Nearby there's the gaudy tomb to the hated aristocrats. Statues of Sir Lawrence Tanfield and Lady Elizabeth lie on stone pillows within an Italianate canopy of columns and arches. Accused in their lifetime of corruption towards their tenants, their ghosts were said to have returned to terrorize locals from beyond the grave. But then seven clergymen trapped their spirits inside a bottle which was flung into the Windrush under the first arch of the town's bridge. Should that part of the river ever run dry, goes the legend, they would be free to wreak havoc again.

It's this type of story that makes me reluctant to leave Burford. But it's gone 1 p.m. and I'm barely 12 miles into a long day, so I retrace my tracks up the hill and turn right onto Sheep Street, resisting the temptation to pop into a quirky sixteenth-century civic building called The Tolsey and two more impossibly perfect pubs. The plan was to follow this road as it climbs back to the A40, passing Kit's Quarries – once a source of a famous pale creamy stone. But then I notice a lane off to my right – narrow and gravel-strewn. It screams "picturesque", it whispers "punctures", but I take it anyway. And, as ever, the road less travelled is the right road. In fact it's probably my favourite of the journey so far; utterly deserted, largely sticking to a contour and offering – between occasional high hedges – yet more views down to the Windrush.

I am now definitively in the Cotswolds – even if no one can ever quite agree on the precise boundaries. I guess Gloucestershire is its heartland (and I'm approaching the Gloucs border) but the rolling fields and golden stone also cover parts of Oxfordshire, Wiltshire, Warwickshire and Worcestershire. For me, the definitive book is *Portrait of The Cotswolds* written by Edith Brill in 1964. For her, it's all about the stone – oolitic limestone – as much for the "gracious, sweetly flowing lines" of the landscape as the distinctive style of the buildings. Incidentally Brill described people from the Cotswolds as "Cotsallers". These days that term tends to attract only blank looks from the locals, though during this journey I'm trying to drop it into conversation wherever I can.

Because I've avoided the main road, I'm in the village of Little Barrington before I know it. From this direction you come across the church before the ancient heart – more idyllic houses clustered around a hollow. It's clear that many a Cotswold village relied on local stone – all those "quarry (dis)" mentions on my map of course. But Little Barrington is interesting in that the "dis" is both right in the middle of the village and clearly visible to this day. In fact the raw material for a number of the stone-mullioned windows and dormered roofs must have come directly from the depression they now look down upon. I get off the bike for a closer look. The pit is long since grassed over with a stream running through it; the wetter ground picked up by bright yellow blooms of mimulus. Three great icons of a village are scattered around the top edge. The water pump, the red phone box – repurposed here to house a defibrillator – and a post box from the reign of Queen Victoria; decades and decades of solid dependability.

But the main reason I'm examining every inch of the crater goes back to London and my starting point – St Paul's

Cathedral. The tomb to its architect Sir Christopher Wren carries the inscription, *"Lector, si monumentum requiris, circumspice"*. This translates as "Reader, if you seek a monument, look around you". Directly underneath, there's a more recent tablet in honour of two brothers who worked closely with Wren. Edward and Thomas Strong came from Little Barrington, owning this quarry before moving to nearby Taynton. In the aftermath of the Great Fire they swapped the Cotswolds for London – making good money as the capital was built anew. Thomas had the honour of laying the first stone at St Paul's in 1675; Edward the last in 1708.

I had learned much of this on a special pilgrimage to the cathedral several months earlier. Mentioning Edward Strong at the visitor desk had much the same effect as "Abracadabra" might do elsewhere. There was an immediate whispered conference among the red-sashed volunteers before a slight but purposeful figure emerged from the huddle and declared "Follow me!" in a manner that brooked no argument.

I'd got myself a personalized tour. And over the course of the next half an hour, my guide taught me everything I needed to know about St Paul's – through a Cotswold lens. I was whisked along the north aisle towards the crossing and down the stairs to the crypt past the crowds looking at the military tombs. At the eastern end of this subterranean world, you'll find Wren's resting place, tucked away in the corner of a darkish alcove, surely unnoticed by the vast majority of visitors.

The newer tablet, installed in 1975, reads:

Remember the men who
made shapely the stones
of St Paul's Cathedral
Edward Strong – Thomas Strong
and all who laboured with them

We will never know the names of those "who laboured with them", but all the smart money is on many a skilled mason having travelled up to the capital from villages like Little Barrington. Alongside, my guide pointed out something I would undoubtedly have missed – a lump of stone, all alone.

"It's an undressed block of Portland Stone," she told me. "In the 1970s they pulled it out of the harbour down in Dorset and brought it here, just to make you think about the work those masons did." The work they did to make shapely the stones.

My whistle-stop tour continued, with me struggling to keep up with her flow of factoids. Then I happened to mention Kit's Quarries – once owned by stone mason William Kempster. At his very name, she turned on her heel and we headed back to the desk where she asked for a large key from another of the Red Sashes.

"This way," she said, a touch conspiratorially.

We walked the full length of the nave down towards the south west tower. And there, behind a solid wooden door, is an amazing spiral staircase – reaching up 88 steps and not open to the general public. These days it's more famous as the "Harry Potter staircase" for its appearance in *Harry Potter and the Prisoner of Azkaban*. But it's more correctly known as the Dean's Stairs, an architectural wonder with each step appearing "to cantilever precariously from the walls" as the author of one St Paul's history puts it. Both this and the doorway outside were built by Kempster. Wren gave him an extra £20 for his work on the latter because of his "extra-ordinary diligence". Cotsaller masons were clearly regarded very highly.

———

I head west from Little Barrington, diverting for a few hundred yards towards Great Barrington just to say that I've crossed Strong's Causeway which was paid for by money in Thomas's will.

Ever since Witney I've been sticking to one side of the Windrush valley; the river to my right, the A40 on the higher ground to my left. It's for a good reason: the main road is a bit of a monster for cyclists and my alternative route shadows it nicely. Harper didn't mind the road as such, but he disliked its elevation, describing it as being "the vacuous roof" of the Cotswolds, empty and bleak:

The heaths and the commonable lands were long since enclosed, their trees felled and the soil turned up by the

> *plough, with the result that in winter the wayfarer sees*
> *the farm-folks, small specks in a world of featureless*
> *fields... whose straight plough-furrows, like the ridges in*
> *a piece of corduroy, stretch on to infinity.*

Perhaps he should have dipped onto my road – now dignified as Route 57 by the National Cycle Network. Certainly he should have made the effort to see Windrush. Windrush the village, that is. I arrive along a road lined with dry-stone walls, climbing towards the church where I take a seat next to another pump. The houses, set back behind well-tended gardens, are as suited to their landscape as any I've seen. Beyond their boundaries, No Mow May has been given a June extension, the verges an explosion of ox-eye daisies and creeping buttercups. At the moment there are no cars, but the odd cyclist whips through, the faint zip of their narrow racing tyres crisply audible on otherwise quiet tarmac. For the rest of the time, a simple silence.

I stretch out my legs, reach for the water bottle and decide that I have reached Cotsalling nirvana. Perhaps it's the precise route, or the time taken to tune in to local detail, or, indeed, the growing warmth of the day, but this place seems to effortlessly sum up all the virtues of the wider district. Certainly it's a great place to bask in the sun and appreciate what a luxury it is to cycle through England at precisely my own pace.

The seat overlooks a small green triangle dominated by five magisterial lime trees. Behind them, the church of St Peter's has some bale tombs outside and a wealth of Cotswold detail within. I particularly like the roll call of vicars. All truly old churches have a small framed list, detailing the 50-odd clerics that typically span the centuries of a medieval parish. At Windrush they go back to Philip in 1230 followed by William of Chiltham in 1282. But it's a tiny parenthesis in the seventeenth century that takes my eye. John Lesley took over in 1624, Robert Rowden in 1647. But in 1660 it's "John Lesley (restored)". Rowden must have been a Parliamentarian, Lesley a Royalist, *restored* to his church in the same year as the king to a kingdom. I feel as if there's an entire novella to be written around that one word. How was that return? Triumphant? To cheers from welcoming villagers? Or sullen and low-key with neighbours divided and feuds still to fester?

———

My next job is to get back on the main road in time for the market town of Northleach. As a result I give the village of Sherborne rather short shrift despite one incarnation of Sherborne House having been built by Valentine Strong – father of Edward and Thomas. Mind you, much of the estate seems to be hidden behind a very solid wall – much taller and more forbidding than the dry-stone examples in

Windrush. Everything else today has been so open and so human in scale that I end up taking this barrier personally. It's almost as if I am being escorted off the premises.

Then, cycling northwards, I start to tackle a brute of a climb back up to Harper's "vacuous roof".

"This is what you trained for," I tell myself as the gradient steepens.

"You're not getting off before that sign."

"You're not getting off before those trees."

"You're not getting off."

When I finally make it – or rather when I finally gather my thoughts and enough oxygen to feel as if I can pay attention again – the A40 startles me with its severity. The broad verges and cycle-friendly pavements of Witney are long gone. It all looked more pastoral in Harper's day. In fact I can tell you exactly how it looked because I've rejoined the road very close to where he worked on another of his sketches. This one shows "a wayside inn" called The New Barn, set back from the road with agricultural sheds beyond. The building remains but is no longer a pub. In fact the whole set-up is more private. A pick-up van is parked up behind a locked gate, but no amount of "anyone in?" hollering gets me any attention.

I hold the book up at the right angle and squint at the illustration a few times. I know it's bonkers, but at times like this I feel I can hear the voice of a cantankerous-sounding Harper in my head. "For heaven's sake, not there, come back a bit and over to the left," he seems to tell me. Bonkers, as I say. Harper's road seems narrower. As is his wont, it's populated by a single figure, on this occasion male, wearing stout boots and carrying a spade over his left shoulder. He might be a farmhand or a roadmender. But it's equally likely that he's a composite "rustic" invented to give the drawing a human scale. ("Entirely understandable artistic licence, Silk," booms my Edwardian muse. "Just get on with it, man.")

On the opposite side of his sketch a small cottage stands directly at the road's edge. Harper confirms in the text that this was the old tollhouse – a rare survivor even then. As for the pub:

> *Those who keep this hostelry are evidently fully alive to its loneliness and to the commercial advantage this remote situation confers, for the sign announces it to be "the last inn for miles".*

Well, perhaps if you're travelling east, but for me heading west, it's a mere 2½ miles to Northleach. Thankfully, a new bypass carries most of the traffic to the north, so I hurtle down the old road in peace to discover that it's a new town from medieval times. As such it was designed around a market place – with burgage plots running off the main streets. Having learned my trade in Witney and Burford, I congratulate myself on spotting a particularly fine example next to Duttons Lane; a small garden for the kids, and then a vigorously healthy vegetable patch full of brassicas, rhubarb, lettuce and tomatoes. Add a grunting pig, take away a plastic slide and it surely looks exactly as those founding fathers would have wished. Its dimensions? Well, according to the tourist blurb it should be 22 poles by 2. A pole being one of those bewilderingly archaic measurements roughly equivalent to 16 feet.

Harper drew another sketch in the market place: the foreground framed by three young trees in full leaf, the church in the background and a distinctive double-gabled building now hosting the post office in the middle distance. But this time when I line the camera up I discover that the view has been ruined by a new building in precisely the wrong place. A municipal loo block of all things.

Still, it's plenty warm enough to sit outside and I enjoy coffee and cake while listening to the stallholders discuss the newspaper gossip as they start to pack up. Another TV star has been suspended and it's all the country has been talking about since I left London.

"Should have got rid of him weeks ago," says one.

"I bet we don't know the half of it," adds the second.

I look around. Northleach contains some fine buildings and the church, at closer quarters, is nothing less than imposing. In fact it's almost heretical to describe St Peter and St Paul's as anything other than a monument to its fifteenth-century heyday when local wool merchants made their fortunes. But, as far as Cotswold towns are concerned, I appear to have left my heart in Burford. For me, Northleach lacks its neighbour's charm despite seeming to tick all of the boxes.

Anyway, for all its listed buildings, it's now arguably more famous for a row of cream-painted council semis behind the high street. They feature in a so-called "mocku-series" called *This Country*. Commissioned by BBC3, it features Kerry and Kurtan as bored cousins kicking around a dead-end town. It's funny, well-observed and very English in its humour. And yes, tourists now turn up on Fortey Road for a selfie.

———

The cyclist heading for Gloucester has decisions to make at Northleach. First, whether to go via Cheltenham or take a more rural route to the south. If it's the latter, then you must further decide whether to trade the directness of the A-road for a quieter alternative – forbidding-looking gradients and all. Back home, I had sought historical precedents. The ever-diligent Harper talked me through both main road options while those who built the eighteenth-century turnpike avoided Cheltenham altogether. With maps sprawled over the kitchen table, I had gnashed my teeth before deciding to go rural and steep.

So, with apologies to Cheltenham, this means that I am now leaving Northleach along a street called The Peep and past a primary school where parents are starting to gather for home time. Then I hit open country along a lane called All Alone – which obviously calls for a photo next to the road sign. All Alone (said to be a corruption of Hollow Lane) soon slices across a dead straight A429 at a scissor-like angle. It's no surprise to discover that this was originally the Roman Fosse Way which ran from Exeter to Lincoln. But the next junction is more unexpected. At first sight I'm simply crossing a Cirencester to Cheltenham back road. But in that lovely Gothic script that Ordnance Survey reserves for such gems, I discover that this is an ancient Salt Way – a special route once used to transport the preservative from the brine springs of Droitwich in Worcestershire to the south in general and the Thames in particular.

This is what I love about cycling. No one could call this lane a tourist attraction, but it has a story to tell. It's what I love about maps too. Admittedly, today is one of those days when even a partially opened Ordnance Survey billows as noisily as a yacht's spinnaker. But a look at the full sheet shows the Salt Way heading north west to south east with a Salperton Park, a Saltway Barn and a Saltway House along its path – historical clues strung out across the landscape.

They're obvious on the physical map, but lie completely invisible to those who would navigate via the tiny screen on a smartphone. A screen where compass points become irrelevant and the blue dot of "me" takes precedence over everything else.

I know. I'm sounding like a Luddite. With every year that passes, I feel that consulting a physical map out in the field becomes more anachronistic. Of course, nothing beats the phone for mobility and GPS-ness. But I've yet to be convinced that the small screen beats the large chart for the wider picture. Certainly spatially. And in this case historically too.

———

I leave the Windrush valley for that of the River Leach, quickly followed by the Coln. The Cotswold kaleidoscope has shifted slightly too: still gorgeous stone, still rolling valleys; but more wooded, and perhaps less picture perfect. Soon, much of what I can see belongs to the Stowell Park estate, normally only open to those who pay to shoot partridge and pheasants. Online, it's talked of as being "ancient oak woodlands and steep banks which produce wonderful testing birds – a true throwback to a bygone age". Well, based on the killing, not as bygone as some of us would wish.

My road offers a mix of steady climbs and precipitous falls. I take a photo of a triangular warning sign featuring a 12 per cent drop – we don't see many of those in Norfolk. Stone walls channel me forward and stereo skylarks fuss overhead. Who needs stucco-filled Cheltenham when you've got Harper's corduroy plough furrows stretching out into the distance?

By Withington the temperature reaches the mid-20s. My water bottle is drunk dry despite a top-up in Northleach and I'm grateful to a Brummie in exile who comes out of his back door holding a beer, to find me begging for a non-alcoholic refill.

"You can have one of these as well if you like, mate," he says.

"Probably better not thanks. Still a good few miles to do."

"Fair enough. Good luck."

But I'm very grateful for his ice cube-infused H2O as the terrain gets wilder and steeper through Hilcot and Upper Coberley. In fact, once or twice I even get off. Giving up like this wasn't meant to be on the agenda till Wales, but hey, I've run out of steam. Glancing at the map to find a nearby slope called "Breakneck Bank" helps salve my conscience.

This no-man's land of not-quite-classic Cotswolds comes to an end when I hit the A435. I could cross it and continue west along more tiny lanes. Instead I turn right to search for the source of the River Thames. At first sight, Seven Springs is no more than a tiny hamlet – a pub on one side of a busy highway and a curiously shaped lay-by on the other. But within that lay-by, the ground falls away around a lightly wooded natural bowl where steps encourage the curious traveller downwards. There, I find a trickle of a stream, emerging from a culvert to the north and soon disappearing under the road itself. Set into the brickwork, a stone tablet makes a bold claim:

Hic tuus
O Tamesine Pater
Septemgeminus fons

Or:

Here O Father Thames
is your sevenfold spring

Springs plural? Harper reckoned he could see a number "gushing forth" from the 175-million-year-old Cotswold limestone, but today, at least, it's less animated and singular. More importantly, is it the start of the Thames? Ordnance Survey declares the source to be some 15 miles south at Thames Head near Cirencester. Others experts agree, arguing that Seven Springs is actually the source of the River Churn – a Thames tributary.

Ah, says Coberley Parish Council on its helpful noticeboard, but *our* source is further away from the mouth of the Thames and anyway *their* springs are only seasonal, whereas our water hurries along throughout the year.

In the end they find a handy qualifier: "Welcome to Seven Springs – The Ultimate Source of the River Thames".

I fill up my bottle again – from the pub, not the springs – and wolf down some rather greasy chips plus a pint of gassy lemonade. It's hardly cordon bleu, but on previous rides I've failed to eat enough on days like this and I'm determined not to make the same mistake again.

Returning to the springs afterwards, I realize that I'm not the only geography geek on an impromptu field trip. Every 5 minutes or so another car pulls up to have a quick poke around. I even spot one couple having a selfie-d smooch in front of the plaque. Young love next to an infant Thames.

———

My legs are starting to give up, but the signpost says there are still 10 miles to go. So I take the busy but direct A436 – despite it being far from ideal for cycling. Thankfully some sort of hold-up limits motorists' speed as we all begin the descent towards Gloucester. The reason for the congestion becomes clear at the badly designed Air Balloon junction. Wedged between two noisy trunk roads, it takes its name from a pub, itself boarded up ready for demolition. Further investigation reveals that the building will be sacrificed as part of an ambitious road improvement project – over the next few years almost half a billion pounds will be spent re-routing and re-designing. The accompanying "fly-through" video talks of it being "landscape-led" with special crossings (they're never called bridges on this sort of literature) for long-distance footpaths.

I love these CGI animations. The sun always shines, the clouds are fluffed up and everyone is enveloped in short-sleeved happiness. Traffic moves freely, couples link arms and there's a mysterious absence of screaming toddlers. Oh, and there's only one cyclist in your 8-minute film, National Highways. C'mon, we're worth more than that.

As I keep the Air Balloon boundary to my right and continue along a narrow pavement, it becomes clear that I am right on the edge of the mighty Cotswold escarpment. This becomes more impressive at Barrow Wake – a viewing point soon to be spruced up as part of the upgrade. The view itself is awesome. The Severn Vale lies in front of me, mile upon mile, acre upon acre. It feels like the kind of place where an epic film would show a feudal queen bringing her heir and saying: "One day, all this will be yours", accompanied by an orchestral score and a swooping aerial shot.

My immediate destination lies directly beneath me – the tower of Gloucester Cathedral standing tall down on the plain. The accompanying panoramic info board tells me the city is now 6½ miles away as the bird flies. But it's the scale of the vista that seems mind-boggling to an East Anglia-dwelling flatlander like myself. I can't make out the River Severn as such, but I can certainly see beyond it. Hills cluster in the mid-distance; the darker and higher ground on the horizon must be from that mysterious country called Wales. The board encourages me to squint, with a single line indicating the outline of the Black Mountains an incredible 44 miles away. I'm not sure I've ever seen such a view from such an accessible spot. Normally you've to climb a

Lakeland fell and hope you're not being lashed by wind and rain. Incidentally, Barrow Wake is described on Google as being "a parking lot in England". Well, yes, sort of. But, tech whizzkids, you have spectacularly missed the point – and some Iron Age history too.

I move on to Birdlip the village followed by Birdlip the hill. Birdlip Hill, all are agreed, is not to be trifled with. Southerners of a certain generation raise their eyebrows at its very name. My mum knew of its reputation. My dad still talks about it. My dad talks about *his* dad talking about it. Harper – probably two generations back from Grandad Silk – went even further, describing its gradient as being among the most dangerous on any major road in the country:

> *The cruel hill has been the death of many, and is now so generally recognized as a death-trap that, besides being plentifully danger-boarded, its beginning is provided with a red lamp, lit every night, inscribed "Cyclists dismount".*

The worst section, he continues, is about a quarter of a mile down:

> *It is generally at this nasty bit that the cyclist who takes it walking feels pleased that he has walked, and he who rides begins to pray. It is round the corner, where the stone wall is, that the rustics generally find the remains.*

Now why didn't I read Harper's wise words at the summit? Well, mainly because it's one of those hills which you find yourself *launched* upon without having made any sort of conscious decision. One minute I'm admiring the pub sign of The Royal George, the next I'm fast picking up speed alongside a sign – placed far too late for it to be effective – warning of a 16 per cent drop.

Aston Hill – the one back near Stokenchurch – has nothing on this. Birdlip is so precipitous that you fear you'll tumble over the handlebars if you brake too hard – but achieve terminal velocity if you don't. Once again I keep an eagle eye open for the tiniest of imperfections in the tarmac, although it's the many studded manhole covers which end up providing most of the jeopardy. They force me into the middle of the road which quickly leads to an unhealthy tailback of impatient cars. Sorry, guys, but you are just going to have to wait. Drivers finally make it past ¾ mile later, one hurling half-hearted abuse out of his window as he does so.

They do love a good gradient here. Just down the road is Coopers Hill, scene of a cheese-rolling competition where people chase a large Double Gloucester down an almost vertical drop – for fun. A week earlier the women's tournament was won by a Canadian who only discovered her victory in the medical tent – she'd been knocked unconscious first.

But I play it straight. Dead straight along the Roman Ermin Way, heading into Gloucester by way of the suburbs of Brockworth, Hucclecote and Barnwood. In theory, orientation should now be straightforward. There's a central crossroads around Southgate Street, Eastgate Street, Westgate Street, etc. The only snag is that Gloucester's entire compass is out by at least 45 degrees. Perhaps it's the Romans' fault. In this rather confusing way I find myself travelling south west on a street called Northgate to reach The New Inn – home for the night.

The New Inn is my kind of place. If not the oldest in town, it's certainly the most historic. More importantly it's the country's best example of a galleried inn. And Harper was in heaven:

> Still the old gables look down upon the courtyard, as of yore and still the ancient galleries, restored from the decay of seventy years ago, run around the first and second floors, very much as they did in that fifteenth century when the monks of the Abbey built the house for the accommodation of pilgrims flocking to the shrine of Edward II.

To this day the ceilings are low – I have the bruises to prove it. The floors sag and bounce – don't bring a spirit level with you. And the corners are artful and ancient – 90-degree joins are clearly overrated. But somehow all this makes it easy to imagine that William Shakespeare paid a visit, perhaps he literally trod these very boards. Modern-day staff help me lock the Jamis Aurora away in a special room alongside at least ten other touring bikes before I head out to explore.

The city centre itself is curiously subdued for 6.30 p.m. on a Wednesday. The reason for this strange atmosphere only becomes clear once I discover Gloucester Docks. In fact I don't discover them, I get completely waylaid by the grand scale of them; a beautiful marina complex surrounded by tall, converted warehouses. Down here, hundreds are enjoying themselves at a whole host of open-air bars and restaurants tucked around two main basins. It's uncharacteristically warm for an English evening and the atmosphere is relaxed. Who knew that modern al fresco dining would go so well with industrial archaeology?

But as I sit down at the Settebello Trattoria to a massive bowl of spaghetti carbonara, I feel there's much to ponder. There is all this life down here while the city centre is left as a sort of netherworld where the homeless are settling in, the unsettled are drifting around and the Deliveroo dispatchers wait for their next order. Is Gloucester Docks a textbook example of how to revive an old waterfront or a warning about the dangers of giving up on a city centre? Perhaps the morning will bring some answers.

DAY FOUR

GLOUCESTER TO MONMOUTH

Day Four

Gloucester to Monmouth

29 miles
2,041 ft of ascent

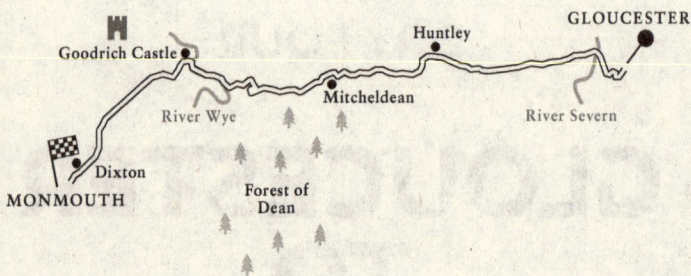

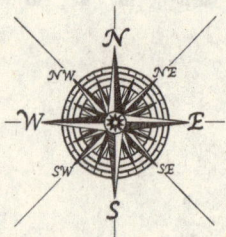

GLOUCESTER

Huntley

Goodrich Castle

River Wye

Mitcheldean

Dixton

MONMOUTH

Forest of Dean

River Severn

N
NW · NE
W · E
SW · SE
S

Direction of travel

The New Inn creaks and groans in the night. Like an old lady in her bedchamber, she is unable to do anything quietly. The sound of restive timber doesn't keep me awake as such, but I do manage to crack my head on a low-slung beam during a nocturnal visit to the loo and later dream that I'm a passenger below decks on some old frigate, gently lurching on the high seas.

In the morning, heading down the many squeaky stairs, I bump into the people those other bikes belong to. They're a cheerful bunch from Chorley in Lancashire – retired or nearly retired by the looks of them. I'm soon directed towards Dorothy and Tony – still cycling well into their 80s.

"You see all these people with Zimmer frames at my age, well I don't want to be like that," Dorothy tells me, with a firm shake of the head.

But she can't hang around because she needs to pack for today's 40 miler. As she goes to help Tony, I am left awestruck in her wake, only hoping and praying that I will be as active in 30 years' time.

After an unsatisfactory breakfast of supermarket porridge, I find myself drawn back to the docks in general and the National Waterways Museum in particular. On a sunny morning, I'm one of the first inside this converted warehouse, soon discovering that you can ignore the N word – its exhibits rarely stray more than 30 miles from the building itself.

The star of the show is the Gloucester to Sharpness Canal. Dug out by manual labour in the nineteenth century, it made Gloucester an inland port by bypassing most of the River Severn's extravagant meanders and dicey reaches. One stretch of the estuary remains so full of whirlpools and quicksand that it's known as The Noose. Enough said.

With the help of swooping aerial photography and assorted nautical paraphernalia, the museum chronicles the canal's rise and fall. I learn about shallow-bottomed boats called trows that plied their trade here – powered by sail when the wind was right, hauled by rope if it wasn't. Volunteers dressed in Victorian clobber welcome me and engage the youngsters. There's plenty to pick up and turn around and a sense of local pride exudes from every scrubbed brick. I tune into that lovely Gloucester accent. Can I call it West Country? I believe opinions differ, but I certainly appreciate the rolling "r" sounds.

I particularly lap up the video memories of four rivermen who learned the ropes on Severn tankers in the 1950s and

60s. The tone is the same throughout: nostalgic for the days before Health and Safety won their capital letters – despite an acceptance that lives were lost as a result. Elegiac too, for a time when the port was a hive of industrial activity.

"And I do mean a *hive*," says one, emphatically.

Back then, lives were ruled by the tide. If that meant being up at 2 a.m., so be it. Fog was the worst of the hazards – the winter of 1963 is remembered with shivering awe. But there were perks. A steady supply of duty-free cigarettes for friends and colleagues – smuggling basically, though none of them use the word. It's more of a twinkle in the eye and a shrug of the shoulders.

"And we never went short of petrol," says another. "Not when you're carrying a tanker full."

These days most of the river traffic is for leisure, as witnessed by the constant chink-chink of the masts among the yachts moored at Victoria Basin. But this morning I happen to find a dredger called *The Severn Lady* hard at work too, pulling up all kinds of detritus from the deep. Scaffolding poles, security fencing, even car axles are piled up on the deck, gloopy mud still glistening.

"Is that you done then?" I shout across to the skipper.

"All done? We've barely started," he shouts back with a smile. "You'd be amazed what people chuck in here."

I need to get going, but I can't leave Gloucester without a proper look at its cathedral, set within a trim close in the quadrant between Westgate Street and Northgate Street. I'm impressed from the minute I walk in. The chunky piers in the nave mark it out as being solidly Norman; the gorgeous fan vaulting in the cloisters is testimony to an expensive fourteenth-century refurb.

The man responsible for the latter lies in effigy within an elaborate tomb. Whether he deserves such a setting is quite another matter. Edward II's reign was as chaotic as his death was horrific. (Precise cause: a red-hot poker up his backside according to the most popular legend.) But the fact that he was buried here meant that the building became a place of pilgrimage – especially after his son set about restoring his reputation. As part of this rehabilitation, Edward III sent London's top stonemasons off to Gloucester to remodel both the cloisters and the whole east end – at great expense.

I climb the 45 steps to the Tribune Gallery. From here the stained glass of the East Window is even more impressive – the size of a tennis court apparently, even if my brain has trouble converting soaring vertical into hypothetical horizontal. Experts say it's one of the most important windows in Western Europe – so innovative, so large and so beautiful that it was painstakingly dismantled during World War Two to be kept in the equivalent of a giant jigsaw box until 1946.

I walk along the Whispering Gallery – so-called because its shape means it conveys even the gentlest of speech a full 20 yards. At the far end I come down another set of hallowed stairs and a return to Edward II. He's lying down, feet up, eyes closed; his flowing hair tended to by an angel apparently in the early stages of a shampoo and set. The "pause for thought" section alongside acknowledges that poor judgement lost him the confidence of his people and the throne. "Can we help others find a way forward in life when everything seems to have gone wrong?" it asks, a touch earnestly.

But overall, this cathedral becomes my all-time English favourite. It gives off an easy magnificence from the height of its nave to the delicate tracery of the cloisters. And I'm always a sucker for royal links. As well as connections to the Edwards, it had previously hosted the coronation of a young Henry III in 1216. Aged just nine, he fell asleep halfway through. Admittedly the ceremony was only held here because of an invasion by the French, but still, there aren't many cathedrals with such a pedigree.

———

I walk the bike back through the pedestrianized centre – thankfully more lively by day than it was yesterday evening. Gloucester is the first place where I start to feel the proximity – or perhaps more correctly the presence – of Wales.

It's not just yesterday's long-distance view from Barrow Wake. One café is offering "Welsh cakes" and there's a Llanthony Abbey down the road. Even the nature of the sport hints in a westerly direction. Based on both conversations and shop displays, I learn that Gloucester doesn't really do football. But they do love rugby – just like much of Wales. After a while I start to imagine that in their very shape, every other Gloucestrian looks like a prop forward. That's a compliment, everyone. Honest.

Still walking with the bike, I eventually find the River Severn hiding behind a lock in the far corner of the docks. Read the old books and you'll learn that Gloucester owes its very existence to this river – because you couldn't cross it any further downstream without resorting to either a ferry or a swim. From that simple piece of geography came all of the city's history – everything from Roman settlement to its modern status as the county town.

I'd always assumed this would be one major bridge – and in my mind's eye it would have been a Gloucester centrepiece. The reality is more complicated and considerably less glamorous. First, all of the riparian action lies to the west of the city centre. Second, the landscape here has allowed a fickle river to change course over the centuries, splitting into three separate channels until the 1700s.

One stream has since dried up, so now there are only two crossings. And cycling across the grazing marshes of the in-between Alney Island proves to be a relaxing, car-free way to leave a lovely city. On the other side, the West Channel is more substantial than the east, with us cyclists getting to use a bridge designed by Thomas Telford while cars trundle across a 1960s replacement.

Glamorous or not, the strategic importance of the crossings did give the city a kind of cachet as the highway to Wales until well into the twentieth century. But not any more. Over the last 50-odd years two magnificent motorway bridges have been slung across the wider estuary much further downriver – each one a triumph of civil engineering. As a result, traffic has gravitated to the M4 and the M48. The river that the Welsh call *Hafren* and the Romans knew as *Sabrina*, has been tamed at last.

———

I'm not sure I would call the landscape to the west of Gloucester pretty, but the views do open up nicely and the semi-circular hills in the distance criss-cross each other just as neatly as in any children's picture book. Stuck on the tarmac in the foreground, I get my head down through Over, Highnam and Churcham, cycling at a reasonable speed. But Dorothy, Tony and Co have already beaten me to the garden centre café in Birdwood. This is in danger of getting embarrassing...

I realize that I am a little ill-prepared for Day Four. And I am certainly less prepared than the Chorley gang whose leaders, over scones and coffee, deliver a steady stream of route guidance as well as travellers' tales. Under friendly cross-examination, I have to admit that I have neither recced this section nor remembered the crucial map. Still, I get my photo of Dorothy and Tony for social media's sake – I'm keen to sing their praises – and we head our separate ways.

I love the chance meetings you get as a solo traveller. And I'm particularly determined to savour them now because later today I'll be joined by friends from back home for the rest of the journey – a complete change in dynamic. I'll gain camaraderie in spades and I'm looking forward to it. But I'll probably be less likely to have chats like this.

———

Perhaps it's the lack of an Ordnance Survey that leads me to turn off the main road at Huntley, slicing off a northern loop of the A40 in a bid to head due west but immediately paying for it with steeper gradients through Little London and Longhope. Mind you, if I'm going to face hills, this is the way I like them – quiet roads with regular bends to disguise and delay the scale of the challenge ahead. I look down on the frame of the bike as I stand out of the saddle to give myself extra purchase for the next climb. All seems to be well, mechanically speaking. I appear to be pacing it better today, almost relishing the rises, certainly enjoying the swooping descents. Pain and gain in roughly equal measure for once. And perhaps a body that has started to adapt to the rhythms of the road. I think back on all those winter miles on Norfolk back lanes. They were worth it, they really were.

I'm now on the north eastern fringes of the Forest of Dean – almost a kingdom to itself if its many advocates are to be believed. Trust me, there's no shortage of local pride in these parts. The Forest's most famous son is the playwright Dennis Potter who once described its culture as being "chapel, rugby football, brass band, choir and pub".

Certainly I've already noticed how prominent the chapels are – we're talking low church rather than C of E – while rugby continues to be a big deal. The referee of the 2023 Rugby World Cup Final was none other than "Wayne Barnes from the Forest of Dean". The world watched as this plain-speaking Forester effortlessly kept some of the planet's biggest sporting personalities in check.

Despite its bucolic isolation – and its very name – this area has an unexpectedly industrial heritage. Believe it or not, it was once home to 102 collieries and 35 iron mines. A winning combination as Harper explained:

> The Forest of Dean is something more than a forest: it is a mineral tract, where iron-ore and the coal wherewith to smelt it are discovered economically side by side, and where, before that use and understanding of coal was arrived at, the dense woodlands served the same purpose.

So don't think of the habitat as being "natural" per se. Between the fourteenth and nineteenth centuries, nearly half of all the iron furnaces in the country could be found here. They may have been dense, but the woodlands were also managed – trees methodically coppiced to provide the charcoal required.

Later, coal mines were also very important. But alongside what you might call mainstream mining, there's also a more idiosyncratic tradition dating back to at least the late thirteenth century.

Back in that age of siege warfare, Forest miners had a nationwide reputation as tunnellers and engineers. That made them invaluable as Edward I battled to recapture Berwick upon Tweed from the Scots. But they were canny negotiators too, insisting that in return for helping him, they should have the right to run mines back home – as long as they could show that they lived locally and had been a miner for a year and a day.

An incredible 700 years later, people are still exercising these privileges. They're called Freeminers and their most evocative memorial lies up a steep lane in the hamlet of Abenhall on the outskirts of Mitcheldean. You have to ask to get St Michael's Church opened, but after a phone call, Sheila the churchwarden is happy to oblige. She's changing altar cloths when I arrive, but proudly points me towards the key exhibit – a stained-glass window installed in 2011. In inky blues and vibrant reds, the back-breaking world of both iron and coal mining is vividly illustrated across nine panels. Seen in this light – literally – the work becomes almost a spiritual endeavour. It was commissioned by the Forest of Dean Freeminers Association and designed by Thomas Denny. But why here, I ask, when the heartland of the Forest lies several miles to the south?

"Well, we've had links with the Freeminers for quite a while," says Sheila, leaving just enough of a pause to make me imagine that the relationship dates back to perhaps the 1960s or even the 1950s.

"You see our font here. Well, they arranged for that to be built after they came back from the Battle of Agincourt."

Agincourt? Blimey.

"So just the six hundred-odd years of links then?"

Sheila allows herself a gentle smile. She's been the churchwarden for 20-odd years, her mother for many before her. Continuity in these parts runs deep. Certainly this window, this font and this tradition appear to be in very safe hands.

———

I keep on climbing to the centre of Mitcheldean – a nononsense working town a million miles away from yesterday's chocolate box Cotswolds. *Downton Abbey* fan Geoff from North Carolina – last seen in Asthall – probably won't make it here. After a bit of a struggle, I find a café in a rambling old building that used to be part of a brewery. Inside, the Covid-era Perspex screens feel a little over the top, but when a cup of tea and a bar of chocolate are yours for under £2, who's arguing.

The staff are friendly and so are their customers. In fact I realize that my conversations have been getting steadily more cheerful for a while. I think back to my previous big bike ride – from London to Edinburgh. At some point during that journey you have to address the issue of the North/South divide. Where is it and how can you tell? For me, it's when people start chatting to you for no apparent reason. And on that ride the breakthrough came in the small Nottinghamshire town of Tuxford.

But on this trip I'm starting to appreciate that it's not really a North/South distinction at all. It's more London and the South East versus The Rest. Or "too busy to chat" versus "why wouldn't you?" I think I was pretty much beyond the Blank Stare Border at Gloucester. But certainly I have breached any last defences this morning. For Tuxford, Notts read Mitcheldean, Gloucs – and the warm welcome offered by The Wellwisher Café – a place where every seat is taken and the banter seems to bounce between tables, regardless of whether people previously knew each other or not.

Just around the corner I find the latest in my collection of town halls. Mitcheldean's is tiny and rather unloved – so ramshackle and draughty that even the parish councillors feel compelled to meet elsewhere. But upstairs there is something pretty much unique: a museum charting the ancient art of... photocopier manufacture.

Now, I bow to no one in my appreciation of quirky museums, but photocopying? Really? Initially, I assume it must be a vanity project thrown together by an eccentric enthusiast. Not a bit of it. It's actually a faithful record of a remarkable chapter of Forest life. Mitcheldean: the Rank Xerox years.

It turns out that the collection of newer buildings that I'd been ignoring to the rear of the café were once part of a factory complex that churned out more than a million photocopiers in a little over four decades. At its height, Rank Xerox employed in excess of 5,000 people, supplying machines across the world.

Among the exhibits: the pioneering 914 machine, the first which could be fed by normal paper and the fabled 813, an early desktop copier – even if it was so heavy it took three people to put it on the desk.

But what on earth are they doing here in the first place? The museum – which is currently only open by appointment and on special weekends – does a great job of explaining why. A company called British Acoustic Films needed to escape the London Blitz and happened upon the abandoned brewery as a safer place to make plotting tables and searchlights for the war effort. After 1945 they manufactured cine projectors before being taken over by The Rank Organisation who, in turn, decided that experimenting with some new-fangled copying machines on licence from America might be worth a go. And getting into xerography early proved to be a masterstroke.

It all came to an end in the early years of this century – leaving only hulks of obsolete machinery and a pool of fond memories behind. But is that enough to justify a museum? It's a point I later put to three of the volunteers who kindly gather to give me a guided tour. Between them Gerald Cooke, Stuart Harrold and Ian Hale racked up more than 90 years of service with the company.

There's a startled pause while they digest the utter heresy in my phraseology.

"Well you're basically questioning the purpose of any museum," says Stuart.

Ian rubs a greying beard and goes for the wider historical sweep.

"All this," and he points at a range of machines spanning the decades, "originally started with a monk in a monastery having to copy things by hand."

"Then you go to the early printing presses, through Gestetner machines, right through to the small printers we've now all got in our own homes. These photocopiers are a crucial part of that story."

They have to be right. At first glance, there is nothing more irredeemably naff than technology we have recently learned to live without. But that's only because we're in the tricky 30-year period before it becomes charmingly archaic again.

In fact, perhaps we're nearly there. Another of the exhibits is a non-working model of the 914. This "faux" version was specially made for the recent Benedict Cumberbatch spy movie *The Courier*. Clearly the film-makers felt that nothing added 1960s authenticity like an oversized machine in shades of beige, complete with clunkily large dials and levers. The original, weighing in at approximately 600 lbs, had proved impossible to shift when the rest moved upstairs a few years ago.

But what happens to the collection now?

"We don't know," says Gerald. "We know it needs to be part of a larger entity somewhere. But where? The parish council aren't interested. There's the Dean Heritage Centre over at Soudley, but they seem to think that history ends in 1945."

"Well something needs to be done quickly, because I'll probably die soon," says Stuart.

"Stop being so bloody cheerful," counters Gerald.

They've got a point. Between them, they've done a super job curating on a shoestring – a labour of love spread over many hundreds of hours. But without much official encouragement and with an average age approaching 80, who can provide a sustainable future for this most niche of collections?

I later contact both the heritage centre and the parish council. The heritage centre say they are aware of its importance but have neither the money nor the space to take it on. The parish council say they are trying to get lottery funding to refurbish the building and are looking to find an alternative site for the museum so that it could perhaps be opened every weekend – staffed by volunteers.

"I understand that it is important to local people," says chairman Janet Keene. "So many people who lived locally worked there. But we haven't got the money, so we're relying on generosity. And at the moment people don't seem to be feeling very philanthropic."

Watch this space.

My forgetfulness in not packing the right map is really starting to grate on me. Salvation comes in the form of Mitcheldean Library – open for business and conversation. Admittedly, on this particular day the ladies are more interested in producing vast quantities of bunting than pure librarianship ("This cloth would only go to landfill and there are a lot of festivals on this summer" says one) but I can still take some crafty photos of the right Ordnance Survey between the sewing in one section and the ironing in the other. (Ten years ago, before decent camera phones, I would have been asking to use their photocopier.)

And then the climbing really starts. The Stenders sounds ominous as a road name and it turns out to be the steepest yet, a grind up and then through some genuine Forest of Dean forest. According to the OS map it's part of "Mitcheldean Inclosure". Look closely and the entire district is split into inclosures – always with an "i" in this part of the world.

The thick dark conifers in the distance contrast with spindly silver birches closer to the road. Somewhere down a dusty track I can hear a chainsaw whining. This is a working forest and the bright orange sawdust detritus from recently felled timber is much in evidence.

Highs and lows come quickly. I fly down Drybrook high street, but can already see the higher ground to follow – open country towards Ruardean. Both Drybrook and Ruardean remind me of northern towns in, say, Derbyshire; places where houses cling to the hillside and drivers are forever changing down to third gear. "No frills, handy for the hills," sang Half Man Half Biscuit about New Mills in the Peak District. I think they'd like it here too.

According to my photo of the library's map, there is a path off the main street offering a more direct route down to the Wye. I decide I could do with a bit of off-roading and persevere even when it involves manhandling the bike over a cramped kissing gate. Never a good sign. Then a farm track disintegrates into lush green pasture tumbling over a ridge and downhill towards trees in the distance. It doesn't feel that public and there's no obvious right of way, but again I persevere. Well, am I persevering or am I being stubborn?

I'm a good 400 yards into the field before I realize that a herd of Jersey cows have emerged from behind one of the copses to head in my direction. In fact they seem quite pleased to see me. In fact they're picking up pace and are not remotely put off by my protestations. I am as uneasy amid cattle as I am with Hyde Park horses. I also happen to have read quite a few stories about innocent ramblers, stampeding cattle and less than satisfactory human outcomes.

For 30 seconds, in the middle of this meadow, there is a stand-off involving me and a bunch of bovines. I shoo, I shout, I swear. It makes no difference, I am comprehensively out-stared. Then a couple of them start to paw cloven feet into the ground. I decide I have no option. I make a run for the far side, manoeuvring the bike so that it becomes a protective barrier rather than a mode of transport. They speed up in pursuit, but adrenalin does wonderful things and I find myself sailing over the top of a hedge before I realize the barbed wire is even there. Phew. Phew and ouch. But mostly phew.

I take a breather and congratulate myself on a narrow escape. It takes a good couple of minutes to remember that the bike is still on the other side of the wire, out of reach and surrounded by my dairy demons. Sadly, but perhaps inevitably, one has taken the opportunity to relieve itself of what looks like several gallons worth of urine over the back wheel. What a cow...

I won't go into every detail of what happened next. But suffice to say it took 30-odd minutes to find a long enough branch to connect with the handlebars and drag the bike within reach. And then another half hour to realize that my only escape route involved a slash and bash through several hundred yards of nettles. Plenty of time for the wheel to dry, if we're looking for a silver lining.

Throughout all of this, I don't see a soul. But I have this sneaking feeling that somewhere, a local or two was having a long, hard laugh at 20 lumbering mammals outnumbering and outwitting one hapless MAMIL, that is, a Middle Aged Man In Lycra.

I make my way back to the road. Within 30 seconds I am flying down Cats Hill towards the Wye. Why oh why did I not take this route in the first place? In the distance, Wales is laid out in all its hill-strewn glory, before a canopy of trees surround me with their shadows on the lower flanks. At the bottom, I get my first glimpse of the river itself and am instantly transported back to an early 1980s scout camp. How one look at a landscape can revive long-dormant memories, I really don't know, but here I swear I can smell the canvas and the campfires of a carefree summer with the 19th Maidenhead scout troop.

I doubt I noticed the beauty of the Wye's serpentine manoeuvres back then. Today I am more engaged. This is the classic, peaceful valley, the river gently winding its way seawards through a fertile hinterland with scattered habitation at a respectful distance on the near bank.

On the other side lies Welsh Bicknor, so-called because there's also an English Bicknor, hidden behind another bend even further in the distance. I'm expecting to cross a national boundary myself, but instead my road takes me into Herefordshire during some easy miles down towards Kerne Bridge. A quick Google over a pint at The Inn on the Wye reveals that this route from Gloucester – originally via a ford rather than a bridge – has a history dating back to Roman times. Instantly, I feel better about abandoning the A40 at Huntley. Guilt at diverging from some imagined True Path is never far beneath the surface on these rides. It only gets assuaged by repeated evidence that my alternative route has a suitable pedigree. Memo to self: just chill out a bit.

The Wye might not be the precise border here, but the presence of a castle on the far bank is proof that I am in a broader Border Country. Goodrich Castle is a whopper, started soon after the Norman Conquest and upgraded in the following centuries. It was occupied by a marcher lord – a noble specifically appointed by the king to guard the badlands. Harper was impressed:

> *Their responsibilities [here] as keepers of the ferry across the Wye into England, were heavy, and their territorial and military importance was in like measure. For Goodrich Castle, built as an advance post above the Welsh bank of the Wye was originally... a rather daring enterprise. Not content with remaining on the English banks of that river, there to await any incursions of the Welsh, its first builders planted themselves in what was Wales itself.*

And arguably helped move the border in the process. Like the churches that I've been admiring since Mitcheldean, it's built of the old red sandstone – in reality more purplish in colour. Truth be told I don't get the greatest of views from this angle – it just sits there on the hill, a brooding presence. But the backward look from the far bank does make me appreciate the understated elegance of Kerne Bridge, set off nicely by the fourteenth-century Flanesford Priory in the foreground.

———

I finally meet up with the A40 again at the hamlet of Old Forge where a truck stop called Jo's Diner lies empty – perhaps defeated by the sheer speed of passing traffic. Certainly, the highway is a different beast to the one I left behind at Huntley. It is now in full trunk road mode – all crash barriers and hurtling HGVs. By trial and error I discover that I can use the old route on the far side till Whitchurch and continue on the near, through Crocker's Ash.

Harper came this way, but he wasn't always impressed. In fact he compared Whitchurch's main street to "an untidy farmyard".

It is in this respect, a foretaste of Wales, and has all the Cymric-cum-Hibernian air which characterizes alike the villages of the Principality and of Ireland.

He gets increasingly rude about the locals the further west he gets. I'll spare you the insults in future. But I envy his era for the way that the highways still melded into the landscape. From the heights of Ganerew, he talks of his road almost doubling back on itself in S-shaped curves – something its modern counterpart couldn't possibly countenance.

In fact, Ganerew is the place where I run out of "quiet lane" options. My photos of the map show a path on this side of the river, but I can't find a way to get down there – even if I could see it. So I end up crossing the English/Welsh border in the least satisfactory way possible – walking the bike along a narrow verge next to the fast lane of a dual carriageway. It's all the more frustrating because I know what I'm missing. Down there somewhere beyond a dense thicket of woods lies a "King Arthur's Cave" and various other ancient sites, some dating back to the Iron Age.

More importantly it isn't particularly safe, so when I finally find a riverside path about a mile and a half later, the Wye feels all the sweeter. A baking hot afternoon has passed its zenith. Cycling feels good again. The only moment of disorientation comes when a loud disembodied voice in a cut-glass southern English accent urges me to go faster. My confusion only clears when a coxed four rowing team heave into view – the stern instructions delivered by a chap with a loud-hailer on a safety boat.

As if to provide a contemplative alternative, a church appears in the most unlikely of places – close to the water's edge and some distance from the village of Dixton which it serves. St Peter's is a little beauty, whitewashed walls kept in really good nick with the exception of a scruffy "skirt" around the base of the tower. The reason soon becomes clear. This place floods – regularly and seriously. Opposite the door there's a blackboard with writing in a range of multi-coloured chalks – as though advertizing a range of ice cream flavours. But it's actually an appeal for donations from the vicar. Because, as he puts it, next to a cartoon rain cloud, "the river regularly visits the aisles".

The evidence is everywhere. There are dehumidifiers balanced on the deep windowsills and a roped-off area where the pulpit should be. The river had done its worst in January with a brass plaque marking the precise high-water mark installed on the chancel arch. It's one of eight at various heights chronicling moments across the decades. Admittedly this most recent line registers below knee height, but both "18th February 2020" and "22nd March 1947" are above my head.

But if the church's interior is charming and its history fascinating, it's the graveyard that I linger in. After the freneticism of the dual carriageway, this peaceful spot is exactly what the doctor ordered. Closer inspection of the information boards reveals a timeline dating back to 735. Wow.

You're not quite out of earshot of the traffic, but I still find a real sense of tranquillity, spirituality even. Put it like this, if my ride was a pilgrimage, St Peter's would be an important staging post along the way.

In the old days a lane would have taken me directly into Monmouth. But it's long since been decapitated by the bypass. Monmouth is both blessed and cursed by this dual carriageway. Blessed because it gives drivers excellent communications to the wider world. Cursed, because it feels cut off from the river that was once its life-blood. Mike Parker, in his book *All the Wide Border*, describes the A40 as being "a thug of a road" in these parts. Certainly I feel as if I've taken a bit of a beating over the last 45 minutes.

I pass a busy Monmouth Rowing Club boathouse, escape via an underpass and manoeuvre my way to the south end of the town, away from the Wye and towards its tributary, the Monnow. I'm looking for the last fortified river bridge in Great Britain. It turns out that you can't miss it. It is as if a vertical section of a castle wall has been deposited squarely across the roadway. This 36-foot-high monster built of – guess what – old red sandstone must have presented a real obstacle to any raider: a study in defiance. If today's town council ever fancied getting their hands on a portcullis big enough for the opening, they could be repelling all-comers by daybreak.

"It embodies the town's heritage as a border fortress and a prosperous market town," runs the blurb alongside. Quite.

I use Monnow Bridge as my ceremonial entrance to the town – all the better for only being open to pedestrians and cyclists. Having crossed the river, I can start to climb the main shopping street – my first bilingual high street of course. Signs point me to *Swyddfa Bost* as well as Post Office, *Toiledau* as well as Toilets. Historical banners hang from the lampposts celebrating the Making of Monmouth or *Gwneud Tre-fynwy*. I've dipped a toe in at the very shallow end of the Welsh language via the Duolingo app in anticipation of this moment. I'm super keen to get my first *Diolch* or *Prynhawn da* out there in the wild, but somehow the opportunity to say "thank you" or "good afternoon" never quite presents itself.

At the top, Monnow Street opens up into Agincourt Square and the eighteenth-century Shire Hall. Built in golden limestone, it knocks the spots off both High Wycombe and Witney's civic buildings, grander in scale and beauty. It once hosted a trial of 14 Chartists – the political reformers of their day. To my surprise the original courtroom is now open as a museum with kids encouraged to dress up and play the role of lawyer, witness, judge, juror or accused. "*Pwy ydych am fod*?" is the question. Who will you be?

The Chartists had crazy ideas like the secret ballot, a wage for MPs and equally sized constituencies. Five of the six demands on their charter have since become uncontroversial parts of our democracy. But at the time, the movement was split between people who were happy to campaign peacefully and others who felt physical force would be necessary to ensure change. On 4 November 1839, that resulted in thousands of people marching on a hotel in Newport which was protected by soldiers.

It was nothing less than an armed uprising, but it failed spectacularly. Approximately 20 Chartists were killed, 50 more were injured and 14 ended up on trial here in the county town. The judge sentenced the three ringleaders to death by being hung, drawn and quartered – the last time that medieval-sounding punishment would ever be handed out in a British court. In the end those sentences were reduced to transportation to Australia – in a similar fashion to the High Wycombe rioters nine years earlier.

Outside, Monmouth shows off its famous sons. Henry V was born here in 1386 and is remembered with a sculpture set into the stonework. Agincourt Square commemorates his victory in battle over the French, of course. Then there's a statue of Charles Rolls holding a model biplane. We may know him for jointly founding Rolls Royce, but he was also an aviation pioneer. Indeed in 1910, he became the first Brit to die in an aeroplane accident.

It's clear that Monmouth has much more to offer along these lines, but time is knocking on and the Norfolk contingent are already mustering. Jim and Nige are first to arrive. Nige, an ex-army man, grew up in North Wales and can speak Welsh, albeit rustily. Jim, very much English, has done the driving, and by the time I turn up, the bikes have already been decanted from his roof to a lock-up within our hotel. Dave arrives later. He too has Welsh roots. His accent might be pure Lowestoft, but his rugby and football affiliations lie firmly with a lot of red shirts and one red dragon. And if anyone were to doubt his allegiance – which I wouldn't recommend – he'd point them to his parents, who he's brought down with him for a family gathering in the valleys, the very heart of South Wales.

Together we enjoy the sunshine at The Punch House on Agincourt Square where I feel slightly discombobulated at being thrown back into Norfolk chat. The Arctic Monkeys played last night at Norwich City's ground and Jim and his family were among the 30,000 hearing them belt out their classics.

"Any good?" I ask, even though my mind feels a million miles from both Carrow Road and Sheffield indie.

"Well they're a fantastic band and we all had a great time, but – I don't know – something felt a bit flat."

They've got to be really good to get past Jim. He's a connoisseur of this sort of gig and will happily drive hundreds of miles to see a decent band. James at the First Direct Arena in Leeds midweek? No problem. What's a few hundred miles for some well-honed lyrics and a decent frontman.

He's also a gadget guru. A classic "early adopter", typically three years ahead of me on everything from software tricks to time-saving tools. And this time he's brought that gadgetry to bear on his bike – of which more later.

Dave makes regular trips to Wales and knows this part of the country well, particularly the nearby stretch of the A40 into Monmouth from the north.

"Steve, I can't believe I'm asking this, but did I see you walking the bike next to the fast lane a couple of hours ago?"

I curse my luck. What are the chances of being caught in that precise 10-minute period by someone coming all the way from Norfolk? Dave is a health and safety specialist who's worked for a number of big-name companies. I know what's coming next.

"What the hell were you doing up there? That didn't look very clever."

What can I say? Sometimes things don't quite work out. Sometimes you make the wrong call.

"Those routes you've planned for the next three days. How are *they* looking?" he adds, with a wry smile and a raised eyebrow.

"They've been done properly, Dave. Don't you worry about that."

And he does know that. Not least because he joined me for the last three days of my trip to Edinburgh from London a few years back. We got lost in Northumberland too. It comes with the territory, I would argue. Nevertheless, I decide now's not the time to mention stampeding cattle. Instead I offer to get a round in to make sure we change the subject.

The Punch House is a fine-looking building with a Welsh slate roof, white stucco walls and black detailing around the many windows. As late afternoon turns to early evening it gets busier – absolutely rammed in fact as the working day comes to a close. Inside I'm pleased to find a favourite bitter behind the bar and plenty of exposed wooden beams above. But there's no sign of a ghost called Charles. Charles was a judge with the power to hang people in cases heard at the nearby Shire Hall. A hanging judge plus a guilty conscience equals a ghostly presence according to local folklore.

Returning to our table, I sit down next to Nige and we compare notes on tomorrow's jaunt – a canoe trip down the Wye.

"You'll have done this before I'm guessing, Nige?"

"Err, yep. Lake Naivasha in Kenya with the army. It was bloody brilliant, although you had to watch out for the hippos."

"Hippos? How do you canoe around hippos?"

"Very carefully."

And before I know it, I've been sent photos of a skinny-looking fella – allegedly a younger version of Nige – whose unit were helping to protect an animal reserve in the 1990s. He'll be alright on the water then.

A meal follows in the cavernous King's Head. It's only Thursday evening but clearly the weekend starts here. We raise our glasses and I manage a mangled *Croeso i Gymru*!

Welcome to Wales.

DAY FIVE

A DAY OFF THE BIKE

Day Five

Kerne Bridge to
Monmouth

15 miles

**KERNE
BRIDGE**

River Wye

Welsh Bicknor

Ye Olde
Ferrie Inn

A40

Symonds
Yat Rapids

MONMOUTH

N
NW NE
W E
SW SE
S

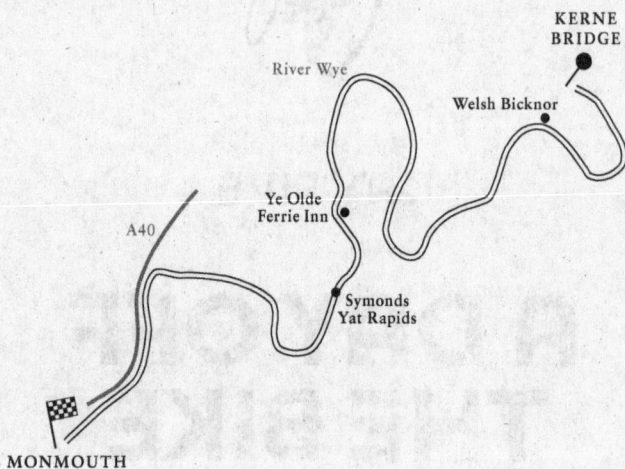

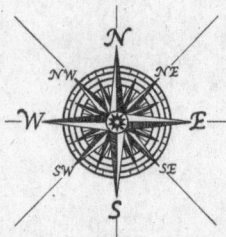

← Direction of travel

There is a tranquillity to life on the water that I don't always find on dry land. And the transformation happens instantly, from the very moment I push off from the river bank. I think it's the silence that is most beguiling, so quiet that my other senses get more of a look-in; the nostril-tingling aroma of freshwater flowing, the sight of alder branches gently swaying. Without consciously trying, I already feel more attuned to the landscape.

Today, the weather is also playing its part. The sky is blue and the clouds wispy – just a flick of an artist's paintbrush here and there. Having been cooped up in a minibus to get to the launch point, I stretch out in the canoe and adjust to the pace of the Wye. Yesterday, as the cyclist rode, it was only 7 miles from Kerne Bridge to Monmouth. Today it will be more than double that as the canoeist paddles. This is a river that has no time for straight lines.

As well as adjusting to the water, I'm adjusting to being with other people. Jim and I push off in one Canadian canoe. Nige and Dave are a hundred yards downstream in another. These three are delighted to have their adventure begin while I'm just happy to be giving my legs a rest.

Our canoes have been hired from Monmouth Canoes – a well-organized yard close to yesterday's underpass. We've gone posh and hired a guide too – in his own vessel of course. I tell Guide Nigel (as opposed to mate Nige) that back on the Norfolk Broads I'm happier in a one-man kayak. He reckons that a kayak should be seen as a hatchback while the Canadian canoe is more of a family estate – with plenty of room for gear. And yes, our stuff is now stowed in watertight containers in front of me – think half-size milk churns in tough polypropylene.

We slip downstream, enveloped by an ever-changing palette of greens. No one else is on the river; somehow we've managed to get this dramatic landscape all to ourselves.

"Kingfisher," shouts Guide Nigel with an arrow of a right hand. "There. About twelve inches above the water. Near that willow. See it?"

None of us do. But within minutes he's found another and this time I do get a flash-frame of electric blue, urgently fleeing to more distant camouflage. I thought I was paying attention before; now I realize I must raise my game still further.

Alpha male talk of a race between the two crews evaporates in the warmth. Comfortable silences alternate with quickfire banter. As well as kingfishers, Nigel points out grey wagtails loitering at the water's edge and goosanders dip-diving, making their rust-brown crests all the spikier in the process. You don't get any of this on the A40.

The sun strengthens. It belatedly dawns on me that there will be little respite for the next six hours.

"You'll need one of these," shouts Nigel, flinging out floppy hats to protect a forehead here and a bald patch there. "It's going to be a hot one."

The Wye is one of three rivers to begin life on the slopes of Plynlimon, the highest point of the Cambrian Mountains – perhaps 80 miles to our north west. A charming Welsh legend depicts Plynlimon as the father, with the rivers as his daughters who must leave home once they've grown up. The Ystwyth was the boldest, rushing to the sea by the quickest way possible – Aberystwyth in fact, on the Ceredigion coast. The Severn wanted to take her time and meet people – nourishing towns and villages en route to the Bristol Channel. And as for the Wye, well, in the words of The Three Sisters project, she said to her father:

> While Ystwyth is wild and Severn seeks culture, I intend to seek beauty and tranquillity by meandering through lush countryside, woodland and forest to make harmony with nature. Creatures will thrive as I flow through the purple hills and golden valleys, creating sanctuaries for them along the way. Wildlife may wander with me, swimming in my path to the sea.

So far so good, old gal.

For the first couple of miles we shadow my road back to Cats Hill. A little further on, the river itself becomes the county boundary. Sitting at the stern, I can switch us from Herefordshire to Gloucestershire with a few deft strokes – if I'm capable of "deft".

"Bit different to the Wensum, Steve," says Jim, pulling his paddle cleanly out of the water and revelling in the silence.

"Fantastic, isn't it?" I reply.

Between us, we have enough cobweb-covered kayaks to get four people out on the water back in Norfolk. And last summer we'd enjoyed a paddle and pint which included both the Broads National Park and drifting past the cathedral in Norwich city centre – a winning combination. The Wensum is beautiful and we do appreciate what we have on our doorstep, but it can't compare with the grandeur of the Wye and the view that Jim's enjoying from the prow of our two-manner.

Signs of habitation emerge on our left bank. It's Lower Lydbrook, a scattering of houses and a pub called The Forge Hammer – the latter providing evidence of the village's industrial past. A railway viaduct spanned this side-valley and now I look closely I can see a buttress high on the hill. Peaceful as it looks, this was once a place of "sooty commerce" where river, road and railway met. Or, as the information board has it – trow, trap and tram. Famously, it was home to a tinplate factory; one photo from the time shows the workers lined up, all flat caps and moustaches, each carrying the long tongs used to push the metal through the rolls – hot work in dangerous conditions.

A few paddle strokes later and all that disappears. My map might show a former cable works on the left bank – old school manufacturing at its ugliest – but a curtain of trees is discreetly drawn across and I'm none the wiser from the canoe. There's a disused railway bridge too, but my eye is drawn to the broach spire of the church at Welsh Bicknor on the opposite side. It sits there all alone save for one building next door – a youth hostel with surely some of the best YHA views in Britain.

Yesterday I had assumed that Welsh Bicknor was in Wales. How very foolish of me. I've since discovered that it's firmly in England – despite the counterintuitive presence of an English Bicknor nearby. The confusion dates back to a time when both counties and countries were allowed to have exclaves – islands of land within others' jurisdiction. Such anomalies were largely abolished almost 200 years ago, but the name lives on.

As we swing north we pass a small real-life island – another variation in the river's story. Subtle changes of wind direction and habitat – a shingle beach here, subterranean rocks causing eddies there – mean that nothing stays the same for long. Kingfishers continue to come and go – but always at a distance.

"You see Nigel," says Jim, indicating with an angled eyebrow.

"Yep…" I reply.

Guide Nigel tends to be to our left and slightly askance, poised like a scrum half waiting for the ball to come out of the pack.

"Have you noticed? He barely uses that paddle."

It's true. His economy of effort is something to behold. Even when Jim and I are in perfect harmony, congratulating ourselves on relatively straight lines, we seem to be working twice as hard.

But then this fella's been on these waters for more than 50 years. His first canoe was put together by his dad from canvas and wood, he'd told me when I first spoke to him on the phone. I think that one sentence was enough to seal the deal.

The river heads south west, passing the *particularly* English Bicknor away to the left. On the right, Guide Nigel points towards iron railings partially hidden in the undergrowth. They stand guard around a memorial to a teenager drowned in 1804. The lengthy script warns parents to be aware of the perils of "the deceitful stream".

The Wye now indulges in its most ornate meander yet – an almost perfectly symmetrical diversion north and then south; the neck of the loophole pulled tight around Symonds Yat Rock. Of all the 185 miles between source and sea, this is the part that you'll find on the brochures, less a gentle valley, more a dramatic gorge.

In the Iron Age – and probably long before – such steep outcrops were the perfect location for settlements; easily defendable against invaders. Then, in the late 1700s, their size and scale helped spawn the very concept of tourism. Grandiose a claim as that may sound, the idea of getting out into the world to appreciate the power of nature was completely novel. A growing trend became a full-blown fashion when the Reverend William Gilpin published his book *Observations on the River Wye, and several parts of south Wales, &c. relative chiefly to picturesque beauty; made in the summer of the year 1770.*

Gilpin didn't invent the word "picturesque" (nor grasp the importance of a pithy book title) but he did help define it. He was forever searching for the perfect composition: a winding river in the foreground, the main body of water in the centre with variation provided by "side-screens" – perhaps sloping hills or thick woods. Cameras had yet to be invented, but there is an argument to say that every time I snap away on the iPhone, I am subconsciously obeying rules first laid down in this valley by a Church of England cleric a quarter of a millennium ago.

I ponder on this as the gorge grows steeper. I guess the similarities don't end with illustration. Those early tourists hired boats for the journey. Tick. They searched out noble buildings like Goodrich Castle and hired locals as guides. Double tick. Visitors were advised to keep out of earshot of the boatmen "so the ear is not strained by the coarseness of language heard so frequently from the navigators of public rivers". No problems with our guide on that score, to be fair – perhaps some mild infringements by his clients.

We paddle north for 2 miles, shooting one girder bridge; the kind of super-size Meccano structure you could imagine army engineers slinging across a war-torn river. Then we begin to loop anti-clockwise, very close to the point where my road hit Old Forge yesterday. Back then – thanks to another veil of forestry – I had no idea all this was so close. On the downward loop the right bank starts to loom large with a scattering of houses perched on the hillside. These properties must have spectacular views, but somehow over-development has been resisted. Is that good planning law or the precariousness of the terrain?

With more than 7 miles under our belts, we're grateful to tie up at the most scenic of riverside pubs for lunch – although perhaps its beauty is enhanced by hunger in the eye of the beholder. Ye Olde Ferrie Inn is a long, narrow, whitewashed building that looks as if it's been added to in a piecemeal fashion over the centuries. "Established 1473" is the proud claim above the door, but we settle down for lunch in a much newer, all-wooden extension. From the outside it's as if a railway carriage has been unceremoniously bolted onto the first floor. But when we step inside we discover a stylish treehouse of a dining room looking down on the river with only the faintest of "new shed" aromas. On one of the roof beams, a stuffed weasel looks down on us, fangs bared, still ferocious in its afterlife.

All this was added after the brutal floods of 2019. The force and volume of the water on that occasion was so strong that two of their pub benches were found washed up 50 miles away at Portishead. In other words, they'd travelled the length of the Wye to its confluence with the Severn, bobbed under both Severn Bridges and finally made landfall approximately 10 miles downstream on the other side of the estuary.

Food and drink arrive in decent quantities – and quickly. We feel we've earned it. As we eat we can look down on a hand-pull ferry – a classic quirk of the Wye. There are now only two of these contraptions where once there were 25 between Ross-on-Wye and Chepstow.

The one at YOFI – the pub loves its funky acronym – is called *The Frog* and looks like a lightweight skip with added railings. Again it's relatively new – the previous incarnation was another victim of 2019 – but the technology remains unchanged. We see the ferryman use a sturdy cable hung across the river to pull his passengers across. It's quite mesmerizing to watch – particularly from our position above the action.

From YOFI, we can just make out more development downstream on the far bank. After lunch, as we paddle on, this reveals itself to be Symonds Yat East, the valley's one attempt at traditional tourism, complete with a pub, an ice cream kiosk and the *Wye Pride* river cruiser offering regular trips from spring till autumn "depending on the river state".

I should pay more attention to both the pub and the other hand ferry, but we are now all more concerned with the Symonds Yat rapids. I hadn't appreciated quite how well-loved they were until this trip. A previous landowner had threatened to get rid of them at around the turn of the century, prompting a nationwide fundraising campaign. Now they are seen as a jewel in the Wye's crown – safe in the custody of British Canoeing.

But I have looked them up. Technically, they are Class II – as in "medium quick water with manoeuvring required", but in contrast to the toughest Class VI category where paddlers face "constant threat of death". As a rank amateur ("white water" and "East Anglia" rarely being put in the same sentence) I would describe them as a decent challenge, with enough genuine jeopardy to make it exciting. Certainly they had been talked up beforehand by Monmouth Canoes as the big moment.

We hear them before we see them, furious water frothing to the left of a central wooded island. A web of cables reach high overhead, like so many heavy-duty washing lines, allowing canoe clubs to suspend their slalom gates for competition.

We have no need for extra obstacles today. But we have donned our helmets and been given our instructions. Pick a line, look for the flat water, keep paddling, don't get caught broadside. Both crews take a deep breath and pile in. Jim and I give it some welly, avoiding both the rocks and too much of a buffeting. I have no idea how Nige and Dave get on, I'm simply too busy trying to stay upright. Suffice to say, we all come through unscathed. Unscathed and exhilarated.

"How many of your customers end up capsizing?" I ask Guide Nigel, as we pull in downstream for an immediate debrief.

"Quite a few. About 30 per cent, I'd say."

"That many?"

"Yeh, but I knew you lot would be alright, you've at least been listening."

We take this as high praise and continue into the most thickly forested section of the river. In fact it's so unpopulated that the imaginative could believe that they were heading into a Canadian wilderness, for all there's a pub and a hotel directly behind us. Everything is on a grander scale than I feel I am used to in Britain – high cliffs with perches fit for buzzards, goshawks and peregrine falcons. The Rev Gilpin certainly couldn't have found anywhere better to promote the daring new concept of nature-led tourism.

———

The river has marked the border between Herefordshire and Gloucestershire for some miles. But now Monmouthshire (and therefore Wales) gets in on the act. So, at the point where the tiny Whippington Brook joins the Wye, there is – at least in the mapmaker's head – a three-way junction which would allow our canoe to span three counties and two countries. In reality, we barely notice the brook, but we do enjoy the idea of a border paddle. As it happens we've split into an English canoe (Jim and I) and a Welsh one.

"You guys stay over there, stick to your own country," I shout in a somewhat lame mock-nationalistic fashion.

Nige and Dave's body language changes instantly. Chests are puffed out, fingers are pointed.

It's made all the more pantomime by the fact that all of us live in Norfolk – closer to Amsterdam than Cardiff.

Guide Nigel wisely ignores all that and pulls us in for another lesson. We need to learn about "swifts" and "edging". Again we take this as a compliment. Swifts are the mini-rapids caused by underwater obstacles. Edging is a technique that allows you to take a more precisely curved route by tilting the canoe and balancing the body. It feels counterintuitive – as if you're going to capsize – but we practise our edging over a few swifts and convince ourselves that we're making progress. At this point I begin to realize how much more there is to learn about the art of canoeing. In one day, we're just scratching the surface.

We're also starting to take this spectacular scenery for granted. The one negative is the quality of the water – it's a dark soup, rather than anything more transparent and life-bearing. Nigel says he's noticed a steady deterioration over the last seven or eight years. "Gin clear" it is not. Campaigners blame the massive growth in chicken farms upriver. High levels of phosphates leach from the farms into watercourses, causing algal blooms to flourish. These, in turn, starve fish, invertebrates and plant life of oxygen.

"A whole ecosystem is under threat. It's getting worse all the time," he says.

Indeed just a week earlier, the health rating of the river had been downgraded by Natural England from "unfavourable recovering" to "unfavourable declining" – prompting a national outcry from conservationists. Scientists found that salmon, crayfish and aquatic plants were all doing badly. Sad to report, the Wye used to be regarded as a classic salmon river. But now even the Wye Salmon Association is warning that the species could be extinct there within a matter of years.

———

The Welsh border abandons us, heading due west to cross the A40 at the same point that I'd entered the country yesterday. Exploring online last night, I'd discovered that there is a perfectly good bike route on the east bank that would have offered a stress-free alternative to yesterday's dual carriageway dalliance. And now I see that it's called the Peregrine Path, I remember the leader of the Chorley gang mentioning it to me. If only I had paid more attention.

On the water, we're firmly in Wales – and on the homeward stretch. To our right, low cliffs provide the perfect burrows for sand martins. Unlike the kingfishers, they are gloriously un-shy, swooping low over the centre of the river in search of sustenance – and fleetingly in front of our eyes. An 800-foot hill called The Kymin comes into view, complete with a white turret near its summit. It feels like Monmouth's personal hill – always there, a reliable neighbour. The A40 gets noisier and the stubby tower of Dixton Church comes into view followed by the first of Monmouth's many rowing teams. It's a pleasantly groundhog way to end our afternoon on this captivating river.

In the evening we meet up at La Piccola Italia where Dave has got half a table full of relatives up from the valleys for a big night out. The Norfolk ranks are swelled by another Dave and an Andy – members of the wider Norfolk gang who don't fancy the cycling but are prepared to travel more than 200 miles for a beer or two. Respect. Welsh Dave's mum tells us of her victory as part of a choir in the 1955 national *eisteddfod* – the annual Welsh cultural shindig. Meanwhile, hearing of my Gloucester route, his dad recalls the days when the A40 really *was* the route to Wales.

"High Wycombe Police used to pick on Welsh cars, they did. This was before speed guns. So they'd come up behind you and match your speed. They'd do you for speeding and then they'd do you for not driving with due care and attention because you hadn't spotted them in the first place."

His fist comes down on the table with relish. The sense of outrage undiminished by the passing of the years.

Later, after some enjoyable trial and error, we settle on The Old Nags Head as our base.

"If we lived here, this would be our local," declares Nige. "They've got a jukebox – and there's AC/DC on it. Where else are you going to find that?"

It is indeed a proper pub – albeit one with a quirky architectural twist. Approach from one angle and it looks like any other corner boozer. Approach from the other and you realize that it's built out from a circular medieval gate tower – a classic bit of border country pragmatism. Why start from scratch when there's some decent old red sandstone brickwork already in place.

Inside, a bloke is handing out fliers to a "Welsh Warriors" night of boxing at Abergavenny later in the month. A lad from Monmouth School is being hailed as "the next Joe Calzaghe" – quite an accolade in this part of the world.

Meanwhile Nige ushers me over to the bar and puts his serious face on.

"Steve, you've got to have a pint of cider."

"I don't like cider."

"You'll like this cider. Remember what Guide Nigel was saying about the finest apples in the country being grown round here. He's not wrong."

Against my better judgement, I give in. I have a pint of fine Herefordshire cider. But I can confirm that even in this most hospitable of surroundings, I still hate the stuff. Proper Welsh bitter can't come soon enough.

Later we walk back through Monmouth's stylish streets to crash out in our rooms at The King's Head on Agincourt Square. Sleep is never a problem on trips like this – it just happens. Tonight there are no aching leg muscles, but as I drift off I just about appreciate the novelty of complaining shoulders and arms instead.

DAY SIX

MONMOUTH TO SENNYBRIDGE

Day Six

Monmouth to
Sennybridge

54 miles
2,959 ft of ascent

SENNYBRIDGE

Brecon

Crickhowell

Monmouth &
Brecon Canal

Abergavenny

Llanellen

MONMOUTH

Raglan

N
NW NE
W E
SW SE
S

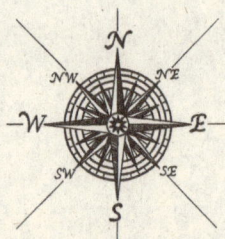

Direction of travel

Back home, early every Saturday morning, we meet up at the war memorial in the middle of our small Norfolk town for a social ride – 20-odd miles and a cup of coffee. We call ourselves the Loddon Mountain Bike Club (Without the Mountains), but we have no constitution, no membership fees, not even an out-of-date Facebook page. Nevertheless one cold morning back in the spring a little bit of history was made within our ill-disciplined ranks. I suspect it will prove to be a slippery slope in the years to come, so I need to put it on record that it was Jim who started it.

He'd turned up for our Saturday Social on an old gravel bike that we hadn't seen for a while. At first glance – a very bleary, 6.45 a.m. glance – nothing appeared to have changed. But on closer inspection a small black motor could be detected directly under his bottom bracket. What's more, wires ran to a shiny new battery on the downtube. But the real giveaway wasn't the tech, it was the look on Jim's face. The usual dawn grimace had been replaced by a beatific smile above his bushy beard. That e-bike conversion kit wasn't pub talk after all. He'd only gone and installed it – at a fraction of the cost of a shop-bought alternative. For the first time, one of us wasn't relying on pure pedal power. We would never call him Jimmy. But perhaps we could now call him e-Jim.

I suspect it was this very day that he'd had in mind when he'd decided to cross the Rubicon. He was very much up for the Big Trip, but a bit doubtful about all those feet of ascent the terrain seemed to suggest. A 36-volt, 250-watt mid-drive motor kit seemed like a decent insurance policy.

I watch him as the four of us set out from Monmouth. Certainly as we cross Monnow Bridge the casual passer-by would be hard pushed to notice. Jim is still pedalling; effort is still being applied, just not quite as much as the rest of us.

"Is it like paracetamol taking the edge off a headache?" I ask, out of the blue.

"You what?"

"I mean the bike. How different does it feel? Are you putting in 20 per cent of the effort, 50 per cent?"

"I don't know, mate. It's difficult to explain."

Truth be told, he's being polite, respectful towards the rest of us; loitering towards the back. Certainly, there's no showboating as we gear up for our first Monmouthshire hills.

There had been a certain amount of "faff" before we set out. Jim had been taking his time. Dave was straining at the leash. Nige was oblivious to both, chatting away at his chirpiest, just happy to be in the land of his fathers. My contribution to the delay was a switch of machines. I've left the Jamis Aurora in the back of Jim's car in favour of a 29-inch-wheel mountain bike. My hope is that this Voodoo Bizango – gangly in size, garish orange in colour – will be more suited to the rougher lanes and occasional off-roading that lie ahead. In my own world for a moment, I wonder if I would have been able to outride those cows on this one – not that the inglorious Ruardean Retreat is still playing on my mind, you understand.

Wales lets us know about its many contours good and early. But a day off the bike has done me good. For the moment at least, these hills hold no fears. Our byroad keeps to the north of the River Trothy, avoiding an A40 that remains firmly in dual carriageway mode. The village of Wonastow doesn't really register while Jingle Street is just a fantastic name – and surely a children's TV show waiting to happen.

We tumble into sleepy Dingestow, crossing the Trothy in the process. A flurry of dunnocks rise as one from a bramble-filled hedgerow on one side while a brace of swallows hunt low over the meadow on the other. You wouldn't believe that the main east–west route came through here, but the smart cream-painted building at the end of a short causeway was once a coaching inn. Now its owners look after another kind of wagon – bright, white caravans lined up as though they're tanning in the sun. A church dedicated to St Dingat looks down from the higher ground and a yellow AA caravan sign swings on its hinges. Nothing much seems to have changed here for a while. Certainly a charmingly tatty road sign still points the way to a station that closed its doors in 1955.

We start to find a rhythm – punishing sharp climbs followed by luxurious descents. Is there anything better than effortless downhill cycling on a warm June day? The lanes are sunken, their hedgerows full of the flowers of early summer – pinkish dog rose on the wax, bright-white hawthorn on the wane. To our left, views open up, nothing that anyone would write home about, just the common or garden beauty of rural Wales.

Until today, I'd been largely making up the route as I went along. But, feeling the responsibility of company, I'd mapped out the next three days on the Komoot app – you can do it road by road, even bridleway by bridleway. In the event, it turns out that only Jim has paid for the premium membership that allows the routes to pop up on a phone. So he becomes the de facto leader, even if his directions are based on decisions made by me, on the laptop, in the spare room, two months ago, in total ignorance of the landscape.

But so far, it's so gloriously good. You'll look in vain for details about the Trothy Valley on any tourist website, but the Wye tributary has vistas to die for. This is another advantage of cycle touring: nothing gets bypassed. And as a result everything gets appreciated.

With barked directions and the odd hand signal for stragglers, Jim guides us safely down from the high ground towards Raglan and *Hen Heol Fynwy* – the Old Monmouth Road. Raglan Castle looks every inch the medieval fortress-palace, but it gets less respect than it deserves because the coffee shop is closed.

"*Diolch yn fawr iawn,*" reads Nige from the noticeboard as we turn to leave. "*Hwyl fawr.*"

His Welsh appears flawless. When I repeat those same words – thank you very much, goodbye – it feels as if I might be taking the mickey. For all that he now lives in Norfolk, he grew up in a seaside village on Anglesey. You can take the boy out of Wales... etc. etc.

We head down to the high street but fail to find a coffee there either – perhaps because half of the population seems to be out applauding members of the 1st Raglan Scouts abseiling down St Cadoc's Church.

"We're raising money for a trip in the summer to the Dolomites," says scout leader Jim Hepburn between quick shouts of encouragement for those nervous of lift-off. "The kids love it and people are always very generous."

Instead we weave our way through knots of proud grandparents and head out into pure farming country. In a matter of miles we pass showrooms for both Claas and

John Deere tractors as well as a cattle mart. Everywhere we look, fertile fields are being enthusiastically farmed.

Beyond, serious hills raise their heads. The conically shaped Sugarloaf Mountain takes its place between the bulky mass of The Blorenge and The Skirrid – the latter a jagged outlier of the Black Mountains. The etymology of The Skirrid is particularly graphic. It is said to have broken apart into *Ysgyryd Fawr* (Great Shiver) and *Ysgyryd Fach* (Lesser Shiver) at the very moment of Christ's crucifixion. Earth gathered from the summit was considered sacred for centuries. Like The Kymin at Monmouth, all three demand a "the" by way of introduction. I like that. To me, the definite article suggests a familiarity and an affection from the people who live in their shadow.

We finally find the required caffeine and cake stop within a garden centre. We're all starving and I take the opportunity to top up the iPhone too. I have become an increasingly brazen electricity rustler at places like this. The procedure is the same wherever I go: a furtive scan of the lower walls followed by the subtle thwack of plug in socket. This is another key to cycle touring: fill up on water, food and power whenever you can.

Meanwhile Dave goes quiet on us and I realize he's tapping away on his phone. Then the penny drops. Despite exhibiting few other Wordsworth-style qualities, he likes to knock out a poem a day on trips like this and the muse is clearly with him – forced rhymes, excruciating double entendres and all. Whether we like it or not, another epic is already in production.

––––––

We lost the Trothy at Dingestow, but soon fall into the valley of the Usk, crossing it at Llanvihangel Gobion. After a dry spring, water levels are low. But the Pant-y-Goitre bridge is beautifully designed for a river in spate. The engineer included a number of large cylindrical holes within the main structure, allowing floodwater to flow through it, rather than just crash against the piers.

If I'd been on my own, I would have come to a halt here, perhaps even indulged in a paddle – it's that kind of river on that kind of day. But collectively the mood is "let's get on with it" and I need to remember that this is no longer a solo operation. The advantages are obvious: comradeship, banter, teamwork. Us four have done a few miles together over the years, we know each other's strengths and weaknesses. Roughly 130 miles over three days holds no fears, but the climbing might – a total of 10,500 feet over the same period.

––––––

On the map, you can find places like Bettws Newydd, Bryngwyn and Llanarth. It couldn't feel more Welsh.

Yet when Harper cycled through Monmouthshire the border was in a different place. A contradiction he spelt out in his own inimical and condescending way:

> By the evidence of our ears, assailed with uncouth and unwonted speech during the latter part of our journey, we might have supposed Wales already entered... and by the look of the mountains which are of a Welsh ruggedness England would long ago seem to have been left behind, but all these signs and portents are nothing beside the fact that Monmouthshire is in England.

In 1905 he was right, technically and legally. But the status quo was wrong, culturally and historically. And the problem can be dated all the way back to a slapdash court scribe in Henry VIII's reign. Henry had decided to incorporate the entirety of Wales into England – a complete annexation. But the dozy civil servant managed to omit Monmouthshire from the list of Welsh counties under the 1547 "Lawes in Wales Act". So despite the strength of the Welsh language in the old days and the obvious presence of Welsh place names through to the present, it wasn't officially part of that country.

Given that all of Wales had been unwillingly subsumed, this administrative cock-up lay dormant until the blossoming of Welsh nationalism in the nineteenth century. Even then it took 100 years of noisy campaigning before the border was formally moved eastwards with a local government act in 1972. Only then did Monmouthshire become indisputably and legally Welsh.

But the prejudice spelt out by Harper against the Welsh language has proved more pervasive. Remarkably, it was only in 1967 – within my lifetime – that Welsh people won the right to present evidence in court in their native tongue; only in 1977 that the BBC set up a Welsh-speaking radio station and only in 1982 that the S4C TV channel followed suit. Laws to further enshrine language equality followed in the 1990s. And it can be argued that it only finally won parity – in its own country, remember – with a further act that came into force in 2011.

Specifically for this trip, I made some rudimentary efforts to learn a few words of Welsh via the Duolingo app. I was amazed at the number of English friends who scorned my efforts as a waste of time and the language as some sort of joke. Harper-style derision is alive and well in England I'm afraid to say – and often from people who would otherwise consider themselves to be "progressive" or "liberal".

Separately, I still find it extraordinary that the two languages have existed side by side on these isles for centuries with only a small smattering of Welsh words jumping over into widespread English usage. Compare that with the equivalents in French, German and Spanish, even a Hindi "bungalow" and Japanese "karaoke" for goodness sake. There ends my *cri de coeur* on behalf of *y Cymraeg*. At least for now.

On the outskirts of Llanover I allow myself a short breather in a picturesque churchyard. I'm still getting my eye in for Welsh churches, but St Bartholomew's would seem to be a classic. A whitewashed nave and chancel with a shorter tower than I'd expect on the other side of the border. Nearby, there's a preaching cross raised on four steps which could date back to the sixth century – emphasizing just how long this has been holy ground. Nearby, a massive sarcophagus holds the mortal remains of Benjamin Hall, a Victorian bigwig responsible for installing the first clock in the tower of the Houses of Parliament – hence Big Ben. He is buried with his wife Lady Llanover who arguably invented the idea of Welsh national costume as well as championing the causes of the Welsh language, *eisteddfodau* (that's the plural of *eisteddfod*) and the playing of the traditional triple harp.

Not a bad historical haul for one very small parish.

"You alright, Steve," asks Dave, as I catch up with the peloton, five minutes later.

"Yeh, just the saddlebag playing up," I reply, having no idea why I am lying.

On the approach to Abergavenny, we start to look out for signs of the Monmouth and Brecon Canal, scanning the lower ground for tell-tale lock cottages or perhaps the odd wharf. After all, canals hug the valleys, don't they?

We soon discover that this one does nothing of the sort. I have got the correct route loaded onto Jim's phone, I just haven't accounted for the gradient. *This* canal is located a considerable way up the hillside, indeed it appears to be virtually clinging to the side of The Blorenge. Getting there requires a steep climb, first through a housing estate and then up a grassy slope which defeats us all – even e-Jim.

But once we're on the towpath, we're in another world. We establish that the "Mon and Brec" is a contour canal – in other words, it was designed to wind its way around the hill at a steady height, minimizing the need for locks and tunnels. It's well-shaded too, creating its own microclimate on what is becoming a hot day.

On the far bank, oak and beech appear well-anchored to the steep slopes. Slightly spindlier versions try their luck on our side. Misjudge the path one way and I'll get wet; miscalculate on the other, and I'll tumble halfway down to Abergavenny. Putting that rather negative thought to one side, the gravelly track is perfect for cycling – car-free and mercifully flat.

At its fullest extent this canal ran from the town of Brecon down towards the Severn Estuary at Newport. It's actually an amalgam of two shorter waterways built in the very late eighteenth century to link coal mines, iron works and limestone quarries – a reminder that while we've seen only farmland and hillside, the heavy industry of South Wales is actually very close. Harper stuck to the road rather than venturing up to the canal, but he was well aware of what lay on the other side of The Blorenge:

> Scarce eight miles across those wild heights of limestone peaks and iron-hard knobs of millstone grit... are the grimy hard-featured collieries and iron works of Ebbw Vale and Pontypool... But nor sight, scent nor sound of them comes athwart that kindly barrier of Nature and Abergavenny nestles, untainted from smoke and dirt, peaceful in a land of flocks and herds.

Oh, Charles, you spoil us.

The easiest way of tracking progress is via the many numbered bridges. We join at Bridge 91 and don't mess about. Nige is setting a pace that's a consistent mile an hour quicker than I am either used to or comfortable with. My Day Two pledge to stick to a chilled-out blanket time – based around that Witney clock with just the one hand – is starting to unravel, for all I realize that we can't hang about.

Thankfully, we all slow down for Bridge 95A and Llanfoist Wharf. Three brightly coloured narrow boats lie moored up with impossibly perfect pot plants positioned either side of each tiller. (One vessel, I notice, is up for sale: "Ideal Liveaboard – £70,000 – sensible offers considered.") On the far bank my eye is drawn to the equally well-restored wharfinger's cottage – three storeys' worth of windows well-positioned to keep an eye on everyone and everything that passes by.

The canopy of trees thins a little here, allowing us to look down on the whitewashed houses and bungalows of Llanfoist proper. The much larger town of Abergavenny is just visible beyond – ruined castle and all. This other world is only accessible via a steep lane, too narrow for the vast majority of motor traffic. Walkers heading uphill use a dank tunnel burrowing beneath the canal. It's all the more atmospheric for the gurgling of a stream alongside – especially as it's called the Devil's Gully.

Beyond the canal, replica wagons on a short section of track remind us that this was once an important transhipment point for pig iron, limestone and coal. In fact if you sent a drone skywards, you could easily pick out the remains of the so-called tramroads which ran between Llanfoist and the industrial hub of Blaenavon on the other side of the hill – perhaps only 3 miles as the crow flies. Blaenavon started as an iron town, but coal mines and steel works soon sprang up next to the furnaces. The Blorenge might reach 1,840 feet in height, but that wasn't going to stand between determined entrepreneurs and their customers. Primitive tracks went up, around and down the surprisingly steep slopes. Each so-called incline used the weight of full wagons descending, to help pull the empties back up. The gradient meant the wagons soon sped up. Getting in the way meant certain death.

Blaenavon's role during the Industrial Revolution means that it is now a World Heritage Site – and that classification extends to both the tramroads and this wharf. As a result, the Blaenavon badge – a heroic image of a miner, leaning on his shovel, staring at the setting sun – gets to be used at the water's edge.

"From here," runs the blurb, "Wales heaved and belched and blasted itself onto the global stage."

Back then, hundreds of thousands of tons of cargo passed under the wharfinger's beady eye every year. Now his cottage is rented out to Airbnb customers and most of the traffic comes from tourists. The contrast between a noisy past and the pin-drop present couldn't be more stark.

More warehouses – and a marina – follow at Govilon Wharf. In between, a succession of cyclists whizz past in the other direction. Eventually their co-ordinated t-shirts make us realize we're in the middle of a sponsored bike ride – dozens and dozens have been taken by coach to Brecon and are now cycling 45 miles back to Caerleon, raising money for a nearby hospice. Further up, a couple of volunteers are staffing a refreshment station – their trestle table piled high with the standard bike fodder – energy bars and bananas.

"I reckon we've had about a hundred through so far," says one, looking down at a bin bag full of blackening banana skins. "All in a good cause."

Abseiling down churches, cycling along canals, a sunny summer Saturday is of course the perfect opportunity for a bit of cheerful fundraising. It's almost as if we're being carried along by the community spirit of others.

I did have a plan for lunch, but it's been scuppered by our lofty position. No one wants to descend to Abergavenny or Crickhowell only to have to climb back up again. Luckily, The Towpath Inn at Gilwern has seen the gap in the market. We take a pew in the beer garden within one of those slightly too cosy wooden booths that future architectural historians will learn to date as mid to late pandemic.

While we're waiting, I have a quick poke around the village. Gilwern is where we say goodbye to the Heads of the Valley Road which has been following us for a few miles. It's no road for a cyclist but, despite that, you'll still find it in my Top Ten of GB roads. It was initially built in the 1960s to connect all of the north/south routes across The Valleys – the beating heart of South Wales. Hundreds of millions of pounds have been spent much more recently to expand and upgrade it, despite the natural obstacles. The result is a highway that takes your breath away with its ambition – even if I do wonder how many thousands of decent bike paths could have been built with the same money (an eye-watering £2 billion in total).

On a more humble scale, Gilwern is where the Mon and Brec resorts to the first aqueduct we've seen, a bridge over the River Clydach – more water tumbling down from The Blorenge. But eighteenth-century engineering endeavour is now dwarfed by a much bigger embankment alongside. The 30-foot-high Heads of the Valleys earthworks are completely out of scale with this earlier work – a fact tacitly acknowledged by the designers who have done their best to tart it up by cladding the sides with local stone reclaimed from a disused chapel.

Gilwern, too, was once home to wharfs and tramroads – in this case serving an ironworks down the Clydach Gorge. Now the cargo is waterborne tourists, with at least two boat companies based here. And it's not just narrow boats. From our height, I can't always see the main road, but when I do, I can't help noticing the number of brightly coloured canoes lashed to car roofs below. We're a long way from peak season, but everywhere I look, people are getting stuck into the serious business of messing about in boats.

A little further on, there's the site of the last major breach of the canal. When you hear of banks collapsing, houses being damaged and a major road closed, you might think of Victorian times. But this one took place in 2007. British Waterways had to spend more than £8 million, first in draining a 16-mile section and then carrying out major repairs.

Back at The Towpath Inn, the landlord had warned us that he was running behind with the food, but in the end, thick, spongy Detroit Pizzas are whipped up pretty quickly. Note to pub kitchens: cyclists aren't overly bothered about fine dining, but we do like quantity and we really appreciate speed. Ultimately, the Loddon Mountain Bike Club are in and out in 30 minutes flat. Compliments to the chef.

———

Somewhere around Bridge 107, we leave Monmouthshire behind for the county of Powys. This was the point where even Harper would have had to concede that he was in Wales. Landscape-wise, it's an odd mix. For the majority of the time it couldn't be more rural, but every so often there's an outbreak of bungalows. I don't know why, but I expected to see ancient cottages rather than 1970s normality.

On country lanes we tend to cycle two abreast, chatting as we go. That isn't possible here. We're now single file, Nige still leading the way with a challenging 15 or 16 mph pace. My rhythm gets broken at every bridge; they're just too low to cycle under without a duck of the head, a micro-adjustment on the handlebars and a squeeze on the brakes. Still, we're undoubtedly getting the miles done.

Not all of these bridges offer easy access to what I now consider to be an entirely different universe beyond the towpath. At Bridge 114, for example, you would have to negotiate four slabs sticking perpendicularly out of the stonework to make it up to road level. Good luck with that very rudimentary ladder if you're walking the dog.

At Llangattock, opposite more bungalows, we find deserted limekilns, much larger than I expected. Where fires once roared from the top of the 30-foot stacks, there's now a peaceful picnic spot, the extra elevation offering views across to the ancient town of Crickhowell. Like Abergavenny it is guarded by the ruins of a castle.

Looking in the other direction, the vast slopes of *Mynydd Llangatwg* and *Mynydd Llangynidr* lie barren and featureless – the OS map shows little more than close-cropped contour lines, the odd sinkhole and some caves. One of the latter was used to hide weapons before the infamous Newport Rising which ended up in that trial at Monmouth Shire Hall.

We can't see the Chartists Cave from this distance. But its very existence is a reminder of how premeditated the uprising was. Thousands of people with desperate living and working conditions were determined to fight for a better life. And I mean fight. Details are sketchy, but we think that ironworkers both made and stored weapons there, before what the cave's plaque calls "the great march to seize Newport". Arguably, these guys wanted nothing less than a revolution. When Hollywood makes the movie, a stirring speech will be delivered underground while red hot metal is hammered on a battered anvil, sparks flying for cinematic effect.

Back in the Usk valley, the layout of the lines of communication has become clear. From left to right, it goes canal/towpath/minor road/river/A40. The canal sticks doggedly to its tree-lined contour. Drivers looking from the other side of the valley could be forgiven for not realizing that it even exists.

But within our world, the landscape is ever beautiful, but always changing – a bit like the Wye, I guess. At Llangynidr we encounter a scattering of locks, each one requiring a spurt of muscle power on the bike in contrast to the usual dead level terrain. In the middle, there is another tourist oasis – a "welcome station" where volunteers help newbies with lock etiquette and more boats can be hired. The maroon of Country Craft Narrowboats ("Novices are our speciality") joining the many multi-coloured liveries that I've seen elsewhere. And here, for once, the gently sloping stone bridge is exactly where I want it to frame the perfect photo. It's an idyllic spot, and I can't help coming to a halt for a quick gongoozle – and yes that is a real word. It means "to idly watch the passage of boats from the side of a canal, particularly from a lock or bridge".

I would argue that it's very difficult not to be a gongoozler hereabouts.

But Llangynidr is also one of those places where you're reminded that the canal is always an exercise in defying gravity. Here, the engineers' job was to cross the *Afon Crawnon*, a tumbling, waterfall-bearing spaniel of a stream cheerfully hurling itself down the hillside at ridiculous speeds. To negotiate it, they built a 90-degree embankment across and around it. Look down from the parapets and we can see a road bridge doing the same on a more modest scale beneath us. At our level, water that would naturally go downhill fast, is being channelled in a different direction by human endeavour. Rightly, both bridge and embankment are listed. In fact you can pretty much follow the path of the canal in this part of the world by tracking the geographical spread of listed buildings. Every bridge, lock, cottage, kiln and bridge is considered so significant that it demands protection.

Further on, the canal enters a low, claustrophobic tunnel. There's no path, so in the old days boats had to be "legged" along – stout boot upon damp brick. According to the blurb on my map, the horse was left to make its own way, meeting the boat on the other side.

Later, beyond Talybont, a succession of drawbridges gives it a very Dutch vibe. These were cheaper to build than their stone counterparts, but are presumably only possible where the canal has a wider footprint. From afar, it's as if each bridge is overlooked by a gangling white crane. On closer inspection you realize that the contraption can fold into a one-sided see-saw as a boat approaches. Timeless technology still getting the job done.

But the most ambitious piece of engineering is saved until last. I guess it's inevitable that a canal overlooking the Usk valley would have to cross that river at some point. And here on the outskirts of Brecon we have the classic aqueduct – one channel of water crossing another at 90 degrees – distinctive enough to attract people as an off-beat tourist location in its own right.

All told, it's no surprise to learn that the Mon and Brec is often voted the most picturesque and peaceful canal in the UK. Unconnected to the rest of the network, life proceeds at its own sweet pace. Perhaps it's helped by the fact that we're within the *Bannau Brycheiniog* National Park – as the Brecon Beacons are known in Welsh. But as far as we've seen, this isn't an area of moneyed tourism or posh hotels, more a scattering of independent hostels and bunkhouses. Prices seem reasonable, its quiet beauty a well-kept secret.

———

Somewhere near that aqueduct I start to run out of energy. Dave spots the signs before I do. First I go quiet, then I fall off the pace, stupidly in denial that anything's wrong. In the end I face a welcoming party next to yet another bridge.

"Steve, you need to eat," says Dave.

I told you we know each other well.

"Jim, what have you got?"

A flattened slice of plastic-wrapped flapjack is produced – of doubtful provenance and age. It looks like someone's bashed it with a rolling pin – not exactly appetizing.

"Get that down you."

It's pretty much an order and – annoyingly – he's pretty much right. Five minutes later I'm chirpy again. The dreaded "bonk" where cyclists completely run out of energy and can virtually fall off the bike with hunger has been averted good and early.

Now alert to the dangers, I also insist on a coffee in the town centre – even though I'm the only one in need. It's partly genuine and partly a desire to steal a bit of blanket time by stealth. After all, Brecon is a significant place, once "capital" of Brecknockshire, even if that old county has now been subsumed into the larger Powys. It is also very much an army town – the headquarters of the 160th Welsh Brigade and "Home of the Army in Wales" according to the large sign next to the no-nonsense stone barracks on the outskirts. The Welsh historian Jan Morris compared these buildings to colonial cantonments in India – the brute presence of a domineering neighbour. It was no coincidence that they had been placed close to "the tumultuous communities of the coal villages" she reasoned in her 2000 book *Wales – Epic Views of a Small Country*. The British authorities weren't going to forget the anger and the determination behind the Newport Rising.

And, exploring the town centre, there is still definitely a defensive/military tang. Streets called Bulwark and Postern, for example; a pub called Rorke's Drift not far from the Gurkha Corner restaurant.

When I last stayed here – at a hotel within the shadows of an older castle at the other end of town – it was winter. The

Usk looked greyer and the stonework bleaker; but the hills and mountains in the distance were dusted with a covering of pristine white snow that alternately shimmered in the sunlight or disappeared completely under scudding clouds. Alluring or forbidding, depending on your mood and their movements.

Today everything is considerably warmer and more cheerful. It's only late afternoon, but many of the locals are already laying down the foundations for a proper Saturday night on the town. Some sort of significant birthday means that large numbers of middle-aged women are already mid pub crawl, nautically dressed and naughtily minded, full of cheeky comments aimed at cyclists' knobbly knees – and worse.

Beyond their infectious giggling, a deep, disembodied baritone voice rings out. Leaving the others outside the café, I follow my ears down Church Lane to find what looks like a wedding party outside the Sarah Siddons pub. One chap, resplendent in waistcoat and suit, is belting out something stirring in Welsh, his fellow guests lustily joining in on the chorus.

Duolingo isn't going to help me here, but there's no mistaking the emotion in the delivery or the pride in the language. I hover on the periphery, too much of a self-conscious tourist to get any closer, let alone ask any questions. I guess I am just happy to soak up this 3-minute window into Welsh Wales.

But time is getting on and legs are getting tired. So the coffee is gulped down and we're soon cycling again. The Welsh name for Brecon is *Aberhonddu*. And we cross *Afon Honddu* just before its confluence with the Usk. The plan was to keep to the valley along some sort of bridleway that I'd found on Komoot. But this soon becomes an overgrown, nettle-strewn non-path. With four of us making decisions, it's abandoned much more efficiently than during any of my earlier solo escapades.

As we climb again, a fine misty rain emerges – a temperature-lowering, aerosol of dampness that we welcome after the heat of the earlier afternoon. (And having previously camped in a wet and un-warm Wales as both child and parent, I never thought I would write that sentence.)

Once again, this feels like an ancient landscape. Around the village of Cradoc, the map shows one Roman fort, two standing stones and a settlement higher up the slopes enigmatically called Battle. Incredibly, there's also an abandoned railway line in the mix. To me, every one of these is an off-road bike track waiting to happen – another key component in my fantasy Go West National Cycle Route of course.

We now have fantastic views down towards an ever more dramatic Usk valley. Stream upon stream (*nant* in Welsh) pour down these slopes. And our road descends and ascends with every one – typically the only habitation is a couple of houses scattered around a bridge. It is at least easy to follow on the map – the pink shading indicating that we're on the very northern boundary of the national park. Still, I look enviously down upon the track bed of the old Neath and Brecon Railway deeper in the valley. One day...

But we're very close to our destination for the night now. A last effort sees us rub up close to an elbow of the Usk before both road and river shoot down to Sennybridge, past the entrance to an army camp set up during World War Two, its buildings very much showing their 1940s lineage.

"Sennybridge ABRO," shouts Nige, his right arm outstretched, as we breeze past.

Clearly we're expected to know this stands for Army Base Repair Organisation.

"All the big repairs for the trucks happened there. I remember it well."

I later unfurl the OS map to find that while the camp is near the village, the Sennybridge Training Area is a remote moorland to the north. The map includes lots of "Danger Area" warnings, not least because this is where live firing exercises take place. Everything from mortars, anti-tank weapons and machine guns get to go bang on this upland plateau.

Sennybridge itself is more peaceful, a charming little village with most of the houses clustered within a triangular wedge of land between the A40 and another road heading south. There are three pubs in the centre, but I've booked us into The White House on the outskirts. This styles itself as a "welcoming and relaxing Guest House", which it is, once you've managed to get past a locked front door made necessary by the absence of a staffed reception desk. But hey, the co-owner is funny and personable and we instantly feel at home, especially after he offers us the use of the garden hose for a bit of impromptu bike cleaning.

Meals aren't happening at The White House this weekend, so tonight's table for four is a bench in the rain outside The Old Stables Fish and Chip Shop, close to the apex of Sennybridge's triangle. One of the ladies leaves the fryer for a minute to take a photo of the four of us perched on plastic bags against a backdrop of industrial refuse bins and calor gas cylinders. But the fish is good and the grins are genuine.

It's the night of the Champions League final, so we're obliged to spend the next couple of hours at *Llew Coch* (The Red Lion) on the high street – indeed, some of this afternoon's urgency has been based around tonight's kick-off time. Safely ensconced around the last free table, Nige is quick to point out the regimental shields lining the walls. Clearly a lot of units have been sent on exercise to Sennybridge over the years. And clearly this has been the preferred boozer for the discerning squaddie.

Meanwhile Dave, the bard of biking, finally shares his completed poem. Somehow he's produced a 50-line monster with masterful couplets along the lines of:

Up and out for brekky at Waitrose.
After some faffing by Jim it's off we goes.

The quality descends as the miles pile up:

After lunch, it's past Crickhowell and Talybont.
Thunderstorms forecast which we don't want.

So that by the outskirts of Brecon we've reached this nadir:

Along the canal we crossed an aqueduct.
Near the end of the day and we were f... tired.

The entire masterpiece gets posted on the exclusive Dave the Bard WhatsApp group. We groan over our phone screens as the rhymes deteriorate. Meanwhile, at a stadium in Istanbul, Man City duly beat Inter Milan 1–0 with Rodri getting the crucial goal.

But the highlight is the pub rather than the football. At least three different generations are enjoying themselves together. It's as if we're in one giant living room where kids are allowed and grandparents indulged – all under the eye of a kindly landlady. Us outsiders are well looked after and this evening I can drink Butty Bach bitter rather than any of last night's apple-based nonsense. What's more, my app tells me that we've done 54½ miles today including a stiff 3,000 feet of ascent. On another incredibly mild summer evening, we walk back to our beds along deserted streets, happy with a good day's work.

SENNYBRIDGE TO CARMARTHEN

Day Seven

Sennybridge to
Carmarthen

46 miles
3,096 ft of ascent

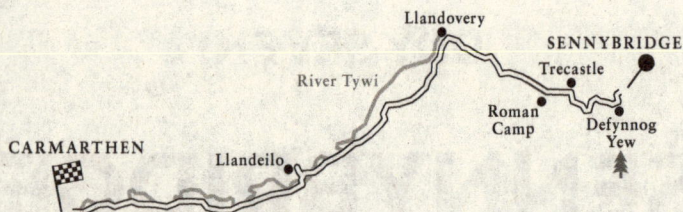

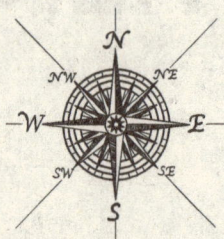

Llandovery

River Tywi

SENNYBRIDGE

Trecastle

Roman
Camp

Defynnog
Yew

CARMARTHEN

Llandeilo

N
NW   NE
W   E
SW   SE
S

Direction of travel

I can safely say that I have never eaten my breakfast in such bizarre surroundings. As I look up from the bacon and eggs, a 7-foot-high giraffe stares back. Painted in black and silver, the wooden animal grips the chains of a chandelier in his mouth, a chandelier that I will bang my head on, if I reach too far across the table for the ketchup.

"That's got to be worth a photo, Steve," says Nige.

I pose gamely for the camera, holding my cup and saucer at a jaunty angle for the sake of the WhatsApp group back home.

"Had a right giraffe at breakfast," runs the caption. How they tittered.

If you check out the reviews of The White House online, you'll find everyone agrees on two things: the welcome is warm and the decor is... "eclectic". From the outside, I guess it looks like a country house. Inside, well let's say it's more Club Tropicana. I glance across from our breakfast table to the bar where elaborate garlands of artificial flowers hang down in creams, pinks and yellows. Elsewhere there's a mass of fixtures and fittings piled up in random corners – mostly ornate mirrors and framed pictures.

Afterwards I wander outside to find a deserted A40. At this hour only the odd farmer in a beaten-up Land Rover is rattling through. The road's silence enhances what is a broodingly beautiful start to a Sunday. I take a deep breath and soak up the aroma of yesterday's rain slowly evaporating off the land – a wonderfully optimistic smell that I normally associate with early morning on British campsites. Looking east, I lap up the views along the Usk valley, realizing that I can trace the profile of the hills all the way back to Brecon. Been there, done that.

Today's plan involves shadowing the main road as far as the village of Trecastle and then taking an old Roman track across a peak called *Y Pigwn* towards Llandovery. It won't be quite as far as yesterday but it will be steeper. In fact the climbing starts within yards of our latest front door – up the road that provides the south side of the Sennybridge wedge, hazy clouds obscuring the top of more distant hills.

But within a mile I insist on a short detour to the village of Defynnog and in particular the church of St Cynog. I'm learning to love the way these buildings sit, squat and whitewashed in the landscape – as though hunkering down, ready for the next storm. Within the porch we find a Roman tombstone dating back to either the fifth or sixth century. According to the handwritten notice above, it is in memory of *Rugniatio Livendoni* – which translates as Rugnatius, son of Vendonius. And, in case any of us needed to brush up on our Latin/Ancient Welsh grammar, the notice's writer has helpfully pointed out that "tio is the Brythonic Genitive".

Who was this chap, I wonder? A Roman, dying hundreds of miles from home? Or a Romanized native, gone posh with a new-style name and fancy inscription.

In any other parish, the stone – for all that it looks like a beleaguered gatepost – would be the star attraction, but we're actually here for something even more ancient. They call it the Defynnog Yew – and some people say it is the oldest tree in the country.

I'm familiar with the idea that yews weren't necessarily planted in holy churchyards. It was often the other way round: the first church was built next to the holy yew – this species being considered sacred by our pagan forebears. But what surprises me is its huge size and rambling multi-limbed shape.

Like the church, it appears broader than it is tall – a solid dollop of dark green which overpowers this section of the graveyard. Presumably it has just kept growing – certainly some gravestones now lie entirely within its substantial shadow – Maryann, wife of Rees Powell of Penybont, laid to rest in 1834, for example.

From inside – and this is a trunk that you can very much clamber into – we get to grips with gnarly boughs heading out in every direction. Some are straight, others twist deformedly. Elsewhere some of the bark appears almost molten in shape and covered with lines of tiny green leaves – almost like hair on human skin. The official description gives the tree's overall circumference as 36 feet with nine distinct stems rising from the base. (Philosophical and rhetorical question: does that mean it is actually nine organisms or just the one?)

Even the most conservative of experts say this tree dates back 2,500 years, but one book puts it at 5,000 or beyond. That's basically forever, right?

At the moment, it's just the four of us scampering around like schoolchildren. But according to a neighbour tending his garden, the tree attracts a regular stream of visitors throughout the year.

"We had a Japanese film crew here a few years ago," he adds, proudly I think. "They were making some sort of documentary."

Today, we find that someone has laid a wreath within a stone circle at the tree's base, while a plastic heart and red roses are wedged in other crevices halfway up. This apparent immortality gives the Defynnog Yew a charismatically mysterious air.

———

We retrace our tracks out of the village and turn left down the narrowest of lanes, crossing the *Afon Senni* before starting to climb a hill that's all too visible in front of us. When cycling, our normal modus operandi is to chat on the flat and shut up when we're climbing hills.

"You know we had to divert to see that tree," I shout, breaking the unspoken rule.

"Yeh," replies someone, distractedly, between huff and puff.

"Does that make it a yew turn?"

"F*** off, Steve."

"I was just wondering."

We're skirting the edge of a 1,247-foot hill that is strangely nameless on my map. From its northern flanks we look back on the houses and agricultural buildings scattered around Sennybridge. Our road keeps winding upwards – narrow, hedge-lined lanes, broken by the odd farm every half mile or so. Meanwhile the A40 sits smugly in the valley – the price of avoiding its traffic is measured in our lactic acid and sweat.

Later, on slightly lower ground, a small bridge takes us over another tributary of the Usk before we return to the mother river for one last time. The village of Trecastle is on the busy A40, with a pub called the Castle Coaching Inn and a holiday let called Coachingman's Cottage leaving us in no doubt about its role in a previous era. But for once my attention is elsewhere: the churchyard next to the chapel – and the first gravestones that I've seen written in Welsh.

Now is probably the time to admit that I'm getting quite nerdy on certain aspects of the language. I would struggle to even order a pint in Welsh, but I'm building up a reasonable vocabulary of the landscape around me: house, stream, mansion, bridge, spring, river. Noun upon noun, I grant you.

But, in my anglophone way, I had assumed that words for things as basic as the months of the year would be like for like. For half of the year I am right. *Mawrth* reads across to March and *Ebrill* to April, for example. But others are far more interesting. Here, alongside the *Ty Newydd* Presbyterian chapel, I find old boys and old girls laid to rest in the months of *Hydref, Tachwedd* and *Rhagfyr* – October, November and December. Who needs months based on Latin numbers when these words translate as stagcall, slaughter and foreshortening? From the rutting season right through to the shortest of days, I'm discovering that Welsh is a satisfyingly visceral language.

The A40 winds its way up another valley – a beautiful bit of non-dual carriageway created in the turnpike era. It's one of those roads loved by bikers, all double white-lined curviness, crash barriers and steep-sided banks. Within one of the lay-bys on the higher ground the observant Hell's Angel will find a monument called the Mail Coach Pillar, erected after an incident in 1835 to warn coachmen against the dangers of drink-driving. In line upon line of carefully engraved capitals, one can discover that a man called Edward Jenkins "was intoxicated at the time and drove the mail on the wrong side of the road" before it careered over the edge, smashing into pieces against a tree 120 feet below.

Incredibly, no one was seriously injured, leaving Harper unconvinced of the need for such a "wayside obelisk". If every near miss was so commemorated, he argued, the verges of the land would resemble cemeteries. But it still stands tall, certainly in good enough shape to make it through to a bicentenary. Jenkins the Coachie's shame lives on for evermore.

———————

In contrast to Jenkins, we spend all of 50 yards on the highway before soberly forking left along the old Roman road, passing a wrought-iron Welsh dragon in a garden and digging in for our most sustained bit of climbing yet. The gradient is always steep, sometimes nigh-on impossible and at various points we are forced to give up and get off. This is going to sound ridiculous, but there is one point where the *extra* gradient offered by a flattened cowpat – less than an inch in height – is enough to make me throw in the towel. Of course Jim is making the most of the "e" bit of his e-bike, but – wisely – he offers generous praise for our human efforts.

Having said that, even walking up these lanes with any sort of gear isn't exactly easy. I'm trialling a Topeak Backloader on the mountain bike rather than a pannier – 6 litres' worth of storage that somehow defies gravity by pointing upwards and backwards from my saddle – as long as I keep the straps taut and its contents well-packed. So far so good on that front, but do I really need all those maps?

When we crossed the Usk we were at 712 feet above sea level. By the time our metalled road disintegrates into a rough track, Ordnance Survey suggests we're at 1,247 feet. In between, we've left the fields behind for heathland, a few weather-sculpted hawthorns at the roadside, some more serious conifers beyond.

The wind picks up and the temperature drops. To our left we can see for miles and miles across to the seriously forbidding *Mynydd Du* – the Black Mountain – well-named from this vantage point. To our right, it's more pastoral, irregular fields on gentler slopes; the A40 hidden deeper within the valley. With the exception of rudimentary fences, a trig point is the only evidence of human activity. We've found Wild Wales at last.

Somewhere over the hills to our south lies the village of Myddfai – home of the finest legend in the whole of *Cymru* in my humble opinion. Like all good myths, it starts with a Lady in the Lake. But, this one ends with surprisingly historical evidence.

The story goes that a young farmer met the woman at *Llyn y Fan Fach* and asked for her hand in marriage. She agreed, they had children and lived happily until he hit her on three separate occasions, prompting her to disappear back to the lake. But she did return on one occasion to pass on the secrets of her herbal remedies to eldest son Rhiwallon who went on to become the personal doctor for the powerful Lord of Dinefwr. In turn Rhiwallon passed the knowledge on within his own family and over the generations they became known as the Physicians of Myddfai. This tradition, we are told, continued for 500 years. And gravestones remembering the last of the line, "John Jones Surgeon", and his father, "David Jones Surgeon", can still be seen in the porch of Myddfai's church. They died in 1739 and 1719 respectively. The ladies who look after the church rub talcum powder into the engraved lettering to help with the legibility, they'd told me on a previous visit. Another bit of local history in very safe hands.

———

On the plateau-like summit of *Y Pigwn* we've now stopped climbing and are more concerned with the quality of the surface. Yes, it was once part of the Roman highway between Brecon and Llandovery; yes, it was the main – indeed only – route until the late eighteenth century. But now it's barely a track, uneven and rutted – much more "off road" than "old road".

The thought that some of these stones were laid down by Roman labour provides historical solace for a while, but ultimately you still feel it on your backside. Belatedly,

I remember to release the suspension on the front forks and thank God for decent chamois cream. We bump along, searching for a line between the ridges and the potholes, but I'm far from complaining. We've made it up to the high ground, amid a panorama of moor and mountain. Here, the air feels fresh off St George's Channel – the stretch of water that lies, as yet unseen, between this corner of Wales and the south east tip of Ireland.

"Standing here on this road 2,000 years ago, you would have been joined by four, possibly five thousand soldiers on campaign," runs the blurb on the info board nearby. "Weary after a day's march [they were] looking for a prominent location in which to set up camp."

The key year for the Roman invasion of England may have been 43 CE, but subduing the natives in this part of the world took a bit longer. The temporary marching camps here date to the 70s. We skirt the very south western corner of their earthwork defences before reaching the edge of what approximates to a plateau, soon looking down onto another vale of gorgeousness – the Tywi valley.

According to Harper, there was a pub called The Black Cock on this westward slope – goodness knows where they found anywhere flat enough. But the ground was too tough for horses:

Up those rugged reaches... it was always necessary for
the coaches to be dragged by teams of oxen; and down

the other side, into Llandovery, [where] the skidpan had
to be put on and the horses led. The road being of such an
extravagant steepness, it is not surprising that it was so
early abandoned when coaches began to serve travellers,
instead of saddle horses.

Imagine you'd paid good money to travel from London, leaving the capital from a smart inn only to find yourself being bumped along here on a winter's night, led by lumbering beasts of burden down a vertiginous slope.

But for us on two wheels on a summer's day, the descent is spectacular – and great fun. Nige and Dave are completely fearless in this sort of terrain. Yes, they're a bit younger than me, but really it's about confidence rather than years on the clock. They throw themselves down a steep-sided, rock-strewn gully of a path, kicking up pink dust in their wake. I know – in theory – that the key to all this is keeping as much weight over the back wheel as possible and staying loose-limbed on both pedals and hand grips. It's the "what ifs" that prove more tricky. At their speed my brain refuses to accept that I won't go straight over the handlebars. Jim is of a similar mindset, so we follow at our own pace. There's no awkwardness between us on all this – and certainly no alpha male nonsense. We've done MTB trails elsewhere; we're well aware of each other's limits.

The sun is now fully out; the path improves in quality, but stays pretty steep. Once it's covered in tarmac all of my "what ifs" melt away. Separately but joyously, we hurl ourselves downhill – 3 miles of non-stop adrenaline. With pretty much zero chance of anything coming the other way, we can reach personal maximum speeds. My Strava graph shows that I peaked at about 32 mph, others will have comfortably exceeded that. But the feeling is more important than the stats. I find myself literally whooping and hollering – at least until I am back within audible distance of the others.

———

"I need these trips for my mental well-being," says Dave, emphatically, at the bottom, coffee in hand.

It's 10 minutes and 1 mile later and we're in the back garden of the *Penygawse* café in the town of Llandovery. He's sprawled on a long grey sofa that looks like it's been stolen from a TV reality show.

"I've been looking forward to this trip for weeks – and that last bit was bloody great."

It's a rare acknowledgement among ourselves of what we've probably all said to our other halves over the years. Cycling, weekly and on occasional jollies like this, is good for us in every conceivable way.

We're not confessional as such – less is more with blokes of our generation – but certainly the odd problem has been teased out on rides over the years. Some idiot at work, the latest scrape one of our kids has got themselves into, or perhaps something as simple as a DIY disaster.

"Well said," I reply. "I needed it too."

We raise our non-alcoholic glasses to the beneficial effects of directing pneumatic rubber tyre against rough Welsh scree. And soon the conversation turns to something uncomplicated. Like football.

Llandovery at 11.30 a.m. on a Sunday is unexpectedly busy. There are the locals, there are loose pelotons of cyclists and there are an awful lot of motorbikes. We're back on the A40 now and these guys will have no doubt enjoyed the run up the *Nant Gwydderig* valley past the Mail Coach Pillar. We'd tried the West End café first, but it would have been a struggle to have found a table among the leather jackets, the Sunday-best chrome and the odd whiff of patchouli oil.

The town itself is still *en fête* from a youth *eisteddfod* the week before. Its brightly coloured buildings are complemented by bunting hanging from every lamppost. According to the programme, 15,000 young people had competed in categories including folk singing, dance, hip hop, public speaking, art, photography, upcycling, poetry and theatre. Five days in all, attracting 90,000 visitors.

All this helps me realize that in a small country, you don't have to be a big city to make an impact. According to the latest figures, Llandovery numbers about 2,700 souls, but that doesn't stop it being a cultural mecca now and the birthplace for some key characters in earlier years.

For example, we've just passed the William Williams Memorial Church on the high street. This eighteenth-century preacher wrote almost 1,000 hymns – in Welsh and English. The title "Guide Me, O Thou Great Redeemer" might not be instantly recognizable, but who hasn't heard the final lines of its first verse:

Bread of Heaven
Bread of Heaven
Feed me till I want no more.

And then the same words for the final line with every syllable belted out with passion:

Feee-ed me til-lll I want. No. More.

These days, the hymn is as well-loved by rugby crowds as it is by chapel congregations. (Dave even managed to squeeze it into his wedding ceremony, he tells me.) Having grown up in a village on the outskirts of Llandovery, William Williams doesn't get a statue as such, but there is a beautiful memorial to him opposite the museum. Only later do I realize that this sculpture of swirling musical notes and floating hymnal pages had been installed as recently as the previous month – no doubt with *eisteddfod* visitors in mind.

More famous is the statue on the mound next to the remains of Llandovery Castle. We look up at a shiny stainless steel knight, 16 feet in height, clad from head to toe in robes, carrying a decorated shield in one hand and the tallest of spears in the other. Most hauntingly, he has no head, just an empty domed helmet secured by means of an ornamental strap. He is the Welsh resistance hero Llywelyn ap Gruffydd Fychan and this tribute was installed on the 600th anniversary of his death.

And what a horrific death it was. According to gruesome legend, he was disembowelled – with his stomach then being cooked in front of him – before being hung, drawn and quartered. When life had finally been extinguished, his body was dismembered; different parts being salted and sent to towns across Wales by way of deterrent.

His crime? Well, the years around 1400 were one of the few times in history when Wales, under the charismatic prince Owain Glyndwr, seemed to stand a chance of becoming an independent nation. Llywelyn had failed to reveal Glyndwr's location to his enemies. In fact he had pretended to be helping the English while leading them on a wild goose chase through some of the most isolated parts of the country. He bought his leader vital time – indeed Glyndwr was never caught – but was punished in the cruellest way imaginable.

"We couldn't get a picture of him," artist Gideon Petersen told the local paper. "But we wanted to portray that spirit with the empty cloak and helmet."

The French have a phrase for parts of the country that appear to be particularly and peculiarly Gallic. And here in this charming and bustling market town, I'm wondering if there needs to be a Welsh equivalent of *La France Profonde* – and whether I've just found its epicentre.

Certainly the Welsh language appears to be in good shape. Speaking to a shopkeeper, I learn that her primary school-aged kids are being taught "80/20". That's 80 per cent Welsh and 20 per cent English. A recent survey had revealed that Welsh speaking was on the wane across the country. But here, while accepting that there's something of a lost generation in the middle, she's convinced that young people are taking up the baton enthusiastically.

Back in the now baking-hot garden of the café, I finish my *bara brith* – a kind of crumbly fruit loaf that Dave's been recommending since Monmouth – and look theatrically at the time. The others take the hint – we're in danger of getting too comfortable in one place. And that is, of course, the cardinal sin of bike touring.

We need to get going.

The A40 turns right at the far end of town and crosses both the railway line and the river. But we stick to the south on the A4069 – the two roads effectively running parallel on either side of the Tywi.

This valley is different in character to the Usk, more open, less claustrophobic with a slower flowing river. As if feeling guilty for our sofa lounging, we pick up the pace along its southern edge, its beauty enhanced by the bright blue sky and soft, luminescent clouds. It may be an A-road, but the traffic is light on a lazy Sunday.

The next village is Llangadog, an old-fashioned high street with a tight 90-degree turn at its heart. We pull in next to the paper shop to allow one monster-sized tractor to pass through. It's soon followed by a succession of four-wheel drives, each towing rattlingly long trailers carrying everything from ride-on mowers to mini diggers. I know it's the weekend, but you get the impression that Teams meetings and working from home aren't so big in this part of the world.

The delay gives me time to look in the window of the *Siop Papur* where I catch sight of cuddly dragons in red, white and green alongside the newspapers; this place is obviously more touristy than I might have guessed. There is a clothing range too, aimed at patriotic babies with one design forcing me into a comedy double-take. Yes, there really is a red and white babygrow – size three to six months – with the motif Feed Me Till I Want No More. William Williams merch. Who'd have thought it?

The drovers brought their animals up through Llangadog in the days before the railways. The number of pubs – and former pubs – that we pass is apparently testimony to those busier times. Certainly as we cross *Afon Sawdde* at Felindre and look across a large swathe of common land, it doesn't take much to imagine large numbers of cattle lowing and sheep bleating.

Plonk me back in the early nineteenth century and I think I'd have fancied the life of the drover. In an age when most people were tied to their own town or village, drovers could wander the country. Under a rule dating back to Tudor times they had to be over 30, married and "known to be honest men of good sufficiency". As well as having responsibility for their walking cargo, they often carried other people's valuables from A to B. Trusted couriers of their age.

I also love the fact that the dogs – often corgis – were sent back from London alone. Their homing instincts were so well-developed that they would "lodge" overnight at the same inns they'd used on the way out. No Google Maps required. Later, when the animal arrived home, the drover's wife knew that her man wouldn't be far behind.

———

For some reason we find the going tough along this stretch. Dave's bike is starting to play up, Jim's left leg is doing the same. I'm sweat-covered, dogged by persistent horseflies and often lagging behind – a combination of weariness and photo opportunities that I see as unmissable but are perhaps testing the others' patience. Though, you can't really go through Bethlehem without stopping for a selfie at the village sign, can you?

Eventually, 12 miles on from Llandovery, we can see our lunchtime location. It's the town of Llandeilo perched on a hillside – not unlike something you might come across in Spain or Italy. Concerns that our road is on the wrong side of the river are assuaged by a pedestrian suspension bridge right where we need it, allowing us to wend our way directly uphill past the railway station. But in the town centre we discover that an annoying number of pubs have a strict "no food after 2 p.m." policy on a Sunday – we're clearly paying the penalty for that overlong coffee break. Hot and bothered, we're in danger of getting "hangry" too until the White Hart Inn comes to our aid with solid roasts efficiently delivered.

Llandeilo prides itself on its boutique shops and multi-coloured house fronts. But I don't warm to it quite as much as Llandovery. Both towns have to live with cars clogging the main shopping street, however what was a minor annoyance there becomes a pain here. There is plenty of life though. During a previous visit I'd watched a rugby international at The White Horse and can vouch for the town's vociferous patriotism – expressed in *Cymru* flags, guttural shouts of encouragement and copious pints of beer.

Back at today's pub, the last of the roast potatoes are dispatched – clean plates all round. Jim pops some painkillers, Nige rubs something medicinal into a complaining knee and Dave has another look at his pedals which aren't always engaging with his hub. All three actions seem to have some sort of effect, so the risk of us turning into a *Last of the Summer Wine* tribute act recedes – for a while at least.

We return to the town centre, catch sight of the trendy shops at last and begin our descent on a road which runs steeply down between the church's two graveyards towards the Tywi. Turning round on the bridge, I suddenly see what all the fuss is about. The town's tourism video focuses on painted terraces climbing the hill, but it's only possible to get a good view from this side of town.

Harper had been impressed, even if things were more monochrome in his day:

> It is a picture in a thousand, this majestic pose... so royally seated on its bold hill overlooking the Towy; the beautiful curve of that arch leaping the river in one span, the whitewashed houses, clinging limpet like to the hillside and tailing away over its crest, the corona of woods, and the tower of St Teilo's Church away to the right.

Once again the main road sticks to the north of the A40 and is rather too busy for our liking. But there's a no-brainer of a B-road, again sitting at the southern edge of the floodplain. Revived and replenished, we're now in good shape to appreciate the beauty of the Tywi at its finest.

This valley appears to have an embarrassment of rocky ruins situated on prominent outcrops – as if for maximum beauty rather than defence. As the drone flies, one could find Dinefwr, Dryslwyn and Carreg Cennen castles all within a few miles of each other. Slightly further afield you will find the National Botanical Garden of Wales, complete with a tropical glasshouse designed by Norman Foster. Perhaps these roads are crawling with holidaymakers in August, but here in June, I'm amazed at how underplayed it all feels – we see the odd brown tourist sign but nothing else.

The castles reflect this land's history as the heartland of the kingdom of Deheubarth – established in the 900s and hanging on till the late twelfth century – with bloody interruptions from the Normans. Harper wrote:

> According to the well-preserved traditions of Carmarthenshire, Dynevor [sic] was the palace... Dryslwyn, the place of coronation and Carreg Cennen Castle the stronghold in the last emergency.

We passed the entrance to Dinefwr by accident en route to our Sunday roast. Owned by the National Trust, it's home to White Park cattle – a rare breed whose lineage is said to go back to those ancient days. Now, as we leave Llandeilo in our wake, we see the castle itself – or at least its most solid part – a circular tower on a wooded hilltop.

A few miles on, Dryslwyn looks even more dramatic. Its remains are "fragmentary yet evocative", according to the experts. Yep, spot on. Only enhanced, I would argue, by the serpentine bends of the Tywi at its feet.

The B4300 wends its merry way westwards, curving in two dimensions, undulating in the third; sometimes close to the river, sometimes drifting away. We pass through the odd small village until the county town appears on the horizon.

If Llandeilo left its best till last, then Carmarthen does the complete opposite. We enter by way of a grand bridge, looking up to what appears to be a French chateau – corner turrets and all. It is actually home to the county council, but with the sun starting to dip in the west, the whole vista surely looks as Loire-like as Carmarthenshire ever can. No wonder this commanding site has previously played host to first a castle and later a jail.

One more nasty climb takes us to the rest of the town centre which is looking a little deserted and forlorn at this hour on a Sunday. But Carmarthen has a weighty history. It is the oldest town in Wales, dating back to the Romans and has always been a stronghold of the Welsh language. In the twentieth century, it was the first to elect an MP from the Welsh nationalist party *Plaid Cymru*. Gwynfor Evans later successfully campaigned for the setting up of a Welsh TV station. And now S4C has its headquarters here.

Our HQ for the night is exactly as I'd hoped. From the outside I would say that the Boar's Head is the classic Welsh coaching inn, an impressive array of sash windows and white stucco – very Georgian. Inside, it's homely with a lot of oak woodwork – again top marks. Some say that there has been an inn on this site since 1610. And there's a bloody legend too. Bull-baiting was apparently common in the town until a Boar's Head landlord was gored to death here, bringing the "sport" to an end. In fact my only complaint is that they've put us in rooms on the top floor

– and my thigh muscles are now aching with every upward step.

There's nowhere within the building to keep the bikes, so we lash them to a mix of old furniture and pallets in a former stable block. Initially I worry about security, but in the end six locks get thrown at the problem, mainly because Jim is the kind of guy to bring a spare – and a spare for the spare. When I return a few hours later to discover that the area doubles up as the staff fag break zone, I'm convinced they'll be alright.

I guess showers should have been our top priority, but somehow the lure of the front bar is too strong. And, honestly, that first pint does not touch the sides. We need it, we deserve it, we pretty much down it. This very room was a favourite drinking hole of the Welsh poet and author Dylan Thomas. If it's good enough for the man who wrote *Under Milk Wood...*

Later we end up at a low-key, friendly Italian called Florentino's where we enjoy heaped piles of carb-loading pasta in a traditional Welsh longhouse. Truth be told we're all pretty knackered. And, looking at the map, there's a dawning realization that tomorrow will be tougher than today. The mood is in danger of getting sombre before another poem comes through on WhatsApp. Dave the Bard has been looking back on our descent into Llandovery. And the rhymes are delivered with his usual panache:

The feeling of joy when we reached the summit
And what fun it was when we started to plummet
The Roman road we followed was full of ruts.
Cycling along it was hard on our... bikes.

Sadly it's all too late for the Llandovery *eisteddfod*. Thank God there's only one more day – and one last poem.

DAY EIGHT

CARMARTHEN TO FISHGUARD

Day Eight

Carmarthen to
Fishguard

42 miles
4,635 ft of ascent

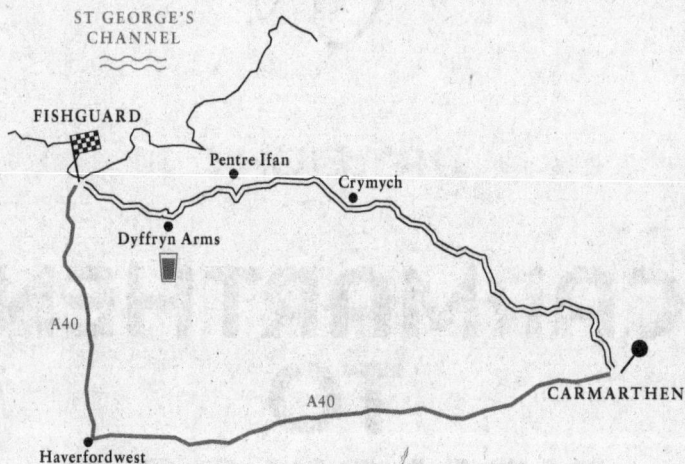

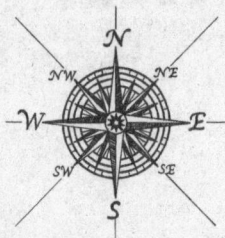

ST GEORGE'S
CHANNEL

FISHGUARD

Pentre Ifan

Crymych

Dyffryn Arms

A40

A40

CARMARTHEN

Haverfordwest

N
NW   NE
W   E
SW   SE
S

Direction of travel

"I've had quieter nights in New York," says Jim with a scratch of the eyes and a shake of the head. We've been "roomies" together since Monmouth, but this is the first time we've faced directly onto a main street. Some boy racer was tearing up and down till the wrong side of midnight, he tells me. It's hardly ideal preparation for what promises to be our toughest day.

I pull the curtains to reveal a wet Lammas Street and better-behaved drivers heading sedately to work. Directly opposite, a beautiful Baptist chapel – one of the finest in Wales they say – hides its classical columns in a courtyard behind more workaday shop fronts; Karizma Barber's on one side, LT Nail Bar on the other. Above and beyond, the hills crowd in, surprisingly close, vividly green and – of course – steep.

I leave Jim to it and head outside for an early morning wander. The Welsh name for Carmarthen is *Caerfyrddin* which can be translated as Merlin's fort. Tenuous or not, that etymology is good enough for everything from a hill on the outskirts to a shopping mall in the centre to be named after the mythical wizard. There are additional legends about a hidden cave within the hill – *Bryn Myrddin*. Some say that Merlin is still sleeping there and will one day emerge to lead Wales to greater glory. I admit that "some say" is doing a lot of work in that sentence. *Bryn Myrddin* lies next to the A40 and I enjoy conjuring up an image of the great man awaking and working out whether to hitch a ride to Llandeilo in one direction or Carmarthen in the other.

Back in the non-mythical present, I walk east along Dark Gate, stumble upon a statue of a portly-looking drover driving his animals safely past Pizza Express and head beyond yesterday's French turrets to Priory Street. Harper made much of an oak tree here which was described as a "most cherished relic". The reason? An old prophecy laid out in rhyme:

When Merlin's tree shall tumble down
Then shall fall Carmarthen Town

The oak was thriving when he came through, but by the 1970s it was both an obstacle to traffic and a withered stump. In 1978 councillors decided to risk a wizard's wrath and get rid of it – despite fiery letters to the *Carmarthen Journal*. One warned that recent floods and snow were just the start: "Do we want Merlin to wage his vengeance on the people who now live in the town of his birth? We don't, so act now and save Carmarthen from the curse that will befall it if we act unwisely."

The compromise was to plant a replacement close by – in a position less likely to annoy drivers. The town held its breath, but the ancient spellcaster seems to have been satisfied. And today, what was once a young sapling is now a respectable enough specimen contained within a circular raised bed, minding its own business.

But who exactly was Merlin? The experts will tell you that he was invented in the twelfth century by Geoffrey of Monmouth, a notoriously unreliable Welsh "historian" who also popularized the idea of King Arthur as part of a wide-ranging legendary landscape involving wife Guinevere, father Uther Pendragon and Excalibur – the sword in the stone.

Whatever the truth, the idea of a mysterious magician born of the union between a virgin and a demon has stood the test of time – with succeeding generations adding their own interpretations. And OK, Merlin is not historical in the strict sense of the word, but he is surely worth some sort of mention at Carmarthen's otherwise excellent museum – alongside the Welsh dressers and the photographs of old coal mines.

"Ooh, that's a good idea," says the lady on the museum's reception when I ask after him. "Write that in the visitors' book. We're always looking for suggestions."

––––––

Returning to our inn, I consider the journey ahead. From now on, the A40 is more often a dual carriageway than not. It heads west as far as Haverfordwest, before turning sharp right for the final 15 miles up to the port of Fishguard. For the last seven days, I've been able to shadow it while rarely having to cycle directly on it. Most of the time there have been enough lanes, pavements and footpaths for me to convince myself that I'm honouring the spirit of the road, if not its precise route.

But my luck runs out at Carmarthen. Back home, after much agonizing, I'd already conceded that I needed a safer alternative from now on. The good news here is that a signposted cycle route heads directly to Fishguard from Carmarthen – and it takes the hypotenuse rather than the two sides of a triangle favoured by the A40. The bad? Well, in these parts, the National Cycle Network's Route 47 is exceptionally hilly. Jim has been tweaking the precise details on Komoot, but even with his improvements, we think we're looking at around 4,500 feet of ascent – way more than we are used to. For comparison, my toughish day across the Cotswolds was about 3,500.

The other difference is its sheer remoteness. Until now, I doubt that I have ever been more than a dozen miles from a supermarket – so near so Spar, as it were. Today in the Carmarthenshire/Pembrokeshire borderlands that distance could easily double. We've already been warned not to rely on finding shops or pubs. As for the frothy wand of a barista coffee machine, forget it.

Our diversion also means that I am abandoning Mr Harper. He cycled on to Haverfordwest before turning south for his final destination at Milford Haven. But even in the early years of the twentieth century, the writing was on the wall. On the very last page of his second volume, he remarked upon a new development at Fishguard, accepting that it would represent the future for the grand old road.

Or, in his own words:

> The loom of time is weaving a newer web, and ere long the railway and the mail-packet establishment will have partly deserted this Haven, much troubled by so many changes of fortune. The Fishguard Railway and docks, now constructing, will change the point of departure... and another chapter be begun in the story of the communications with Ireland.

Importantly for me – but to no one else in the world – my destination therefore has his blessing.

Back at the Boar's Head, our early morning drill is to max out on the breakfast fry-up, clean up the bikes – which are safe but covered in pigeon droppings – and stock up on supplies at Tesco, before heading out into the rain.

My Ordnance Survey shows the terrain to the north of the town as a swirl of wobbly concentric circles indicating conical summit upon conical summit. Take away the overlaying text and these contours would make a beautiful piece of abstract art. A mock Matisse perhaps – ochre brown on pale cream, grid squares optional.

Within a few hundred yards, the first bit of gradient kicks in. We are quickly grinding away in a low gear past the smart, grey-painted semis so typical of Welsh suburbia.

Minutes later Carmarthen is forgotten entirely as the climbing intensifies around the village of *Ffynnon Ddrain*, where a couple of wooded switchbacks wouldn't look out of place on a Tour de France highlights reel – at least in my mind's eye.

Certainly my water bottle is more than half empty within 5 miles. I'm determined not to run out today, so decide to throw myself upon the mercy of any householder I find outside in their garden. This is of no surprise to the first chap I accost, who says he often provides refills for cyclists. But he's shocked to hear that we are neither German nor heading for Ireland.

"So you've only come from London, have you?"

"Err, yeh, 'fraid so."

Only London? No wonder the water comes from the outside tap.

Further on, another Good Samaritan is a farmer about to leave home on his quad bike. It's hard to hear with the white noise of multiple lambs bleating horribly in the neighbouring field.

"They've just been separated from the ewes," he tells me. "Give them twenty-four hours and they'll be alright."

But when we compare notes on just how far we can see over the sprawling fields, boy, do I struggle with locations. In the hands of a native Welsh speaker, place names are difficult to keep in my head without a finger pointed at a map.

Talking of language, the most interesting border in these parts is the one that *isn't* on any official map – the so-called Landsker Line. South of it, in this corner of Wales, people mostly spoke and speak English. To the north it was – and is – Welsh.

The division can be dated back to the eleventh century when a group of settlers from Flanders were "planted" here by the English Crown, sweeping native people out in a process we would now call ethnic cleansing. Over the centuries, runs the theory, these Flemings gradually lost their own customs, taking to English rather than Welsh – both in terms of language and support on the battlefield.

Some of the details are disputed by historians. But whatever the precise truth, modern graphs mapping the density of the Welsh-speaking population still testify to a sharp linguistic divide. We're solidly in the Welsh-speaking area up here, but the A40 will cross the Landsker Line between Carmarthen and Haverfordwest. Harper knew his history and noticed the difference on the map:

The place names – those unfailing tests – begin as Narbeth is left behind, to mirror this long-standing foreign occupation as the Welsh would call it; English names at first alternating with Welsh, and finally by the time Haverfordwest is reached, reigning alone. They are almost exclusive[ly]... names ending with "ton" such as Haroldston, Johnston, Herbrandston, Robeston and Steynton, and mark, more clearly than anything else, that ancient racial cleavage.

That part of the world is now known as "Little England beyond Wales". It's incredible to think that events from 900-odd years ago continue to leave their mark.

————

Back on the road there are sweeping downs, but they tend to be outnumbered two to one by the relentless ups. Sometimes we feel hemmed in, such is the density and height of the hedgerows. But then we'll crest a hill to find an expansive view unfolding, acre upon acre. I look for the sea, but it's still too far to the north. Instead, on a ridge in the distance, a stunted oak leans doggedly; the paucity of the foliage on one side clearly showing the direction of the prevailing wind.

On the outskirts of Talog I discover that I have been spat out of the back of the Team Loddon peloton as I dawdle down into a wooded valley which seems to attract only the most lightly dappled of sunlight. On the left-hand side there is a steep bank, perhaps 12 feet tall, covered in a thick layer of green moss – a vast velvet curtain draped across the hillside. Something makes me come to a halt, the better to take it in, when a line from Jan Morris's book comes straight back to my mind. Trying to sum up the physical geography of her beloved country, she argued that the sensation of rural Wales can be concentrated on a very small area as long as it is: "tufted and ferned and mossed enough… if its slab of stone is sufficiently mottled, if the earth is properly peaty and the air slightly mushroomy."

Using all of my senses, this winding road ticks all of her boxes. And thanks to the serendipity of cycling, I've just found another bit of "profound" Wales, even if I couldn't have appreciated it in those terms without her help. It's a magical place where I'm keen to loiter – even as I realize that I am holding up the others.

———

We regroup in the hamlet of Talog – which appears to be more a collection of working buildings than a village as such – and continue to make steady if unspectacular progress. We've decided that we are actually enjoying the solitude by way of contrast to yesterday.

Traffic? What traffic? Towns? What towns?

But there are tiny villages, many clustered around bridges across fast-flowing streams. One called Pen-y-bont is perhaps typical. First, there's a house on a hill by way of warning, then another, next to the most stubborn of small grey churches – not even a tower, just a modest bellcote and porch. A pair of semi-detached cottages appear unlived in – certainly you'd be hard pushed to get through either of the front gardens without a scythe or at least a pair of sturdy loppers.

But these are just fleeting images. I barely have time to take them in before a triangular sign after the last farmyard warns of an 18 per cent descent towards what turns out to be the heart of the place. As well as smartly painted houses there is a former school repurposed as a community centre on one bank of the *Dewi Fawr* stream while the tall profile of a non-conformist chapel looms on the other.

All told, there are probably no more than a dozen properties in the centre of Pen-y-bont, together with roughly the same number of farm sheds, some of which are practically wedged against the hillside for extra shelter. We don't see a soul either in the valley or up on the ridge. And even on this most benign of days, the wind howls around. God knows what it's like during a winter gale.

So far, the small red-on-blue cycle route signs have been reliable; sparingly used, but reliable. Here they direct us to the right of the old school along our narrowest lane yet. It's the kind of sign that makes you think: "Really?"

The tougher types of weed are defying the decaying tarmac in the middle. The hedgerows are even thicker than in the Trothy valley. I'm not sure lack of rainfall has been so much of a problem in these parts – or maybe the tree cover is heavier. Soon a couple of particularly brutal switchbacks leave us gasping for breath. In fact those of us relying on pedal power are now more often to be found walking than cycling. And the other member of the team is sensible enough to keep quiet while we do so.

Along the leafy lanes, foxgloves thrust themselves towards the middle of the tarmac in a bid for more sunlight. If they were a little more regular and slightly taller, you could call them an honour guard. Give them till August and perhaps they will be. Apart from the odd ammoniacal waft from a cow shed, the aroma is of a vigorously healthy summer. Green, green, green. Growth, growth, growth.

Trelech is a little busier, with some modern housing. Dinas is more old school, a yellow squiggle of a road diving into and out of another precipitous valley. Tegryn has a school and is – in the jargon – a classic "hilltop linear village".

The landscape relaxes a little and the hedges withdraw too. It is now just extremely hilly rather than extreme hills. Might we just have weathered the worst? And is this still Carmarthenshire or have we made it to Pembrokeshire? A few miles further on, we find a rare roadside seat which quickly becomes a table for our combined lunches. Jim pulls some Tesco sushi out of the pannier – to the amusement of the rest of us. It hardly seems to square with the day's "roughing it" vibe – a fact he is reminded of for the rest of the day.

And while one of us may be having a metropolitan meal, none of us are getting delayed by other fripperies like sofas or flat whites. As a result we're finding a better balance – 5 minutes to catch our breath on the many summits, but no more. Satisfyingly, we're making faster progress than we might have thought when we considered our route at Florentino's last night.

The odd car overtakes us in two pukka villages, both grand enough to have pubs, although – reasonably enough – they're not open on a Monday lunchtime. Crymych also possesses a garage, an A-road, and – despite the warnings from people in Carmarthen – shops.

We're now approaching the Pembrokeshire Coast National Park in general and the wild moorland of *Mynydd Preseli* in particular. The Preseli Mountains (less than 1,800 feet high if we're being fussy) have a mystery all of their own. Ancient tracks run across them, standing stones appear liberally scattered. And, most tantalizingly of all, some of the very building blocks for Stonehenge were transported from here thousands of years ago.

In 2024, new research revealed that the largest of the so-called bluestones was actually from Scotland. But the majority came from these mountains – again, an awfully long way from their final resting place in Wiltshire. The Welsh breakthrough came in the 1920s, but it's only in the last decade that they have pinpointed the precise location. To some people's surprise, the so-called "megalith quarry" is actually on the north side of the Preselis rather than the south, undermining a theory that the stones would have been dragged to Milford Haven and then shipped up the Bristol Channel before somehow being dragged across to Salisbury Plain.

Instead, insisted the academic leading the dig, they would have had to go up to St David's Head or directly overland. To my delight the news release from the time then quotes Professor Parker Pearson saying the latter route "through the valleys along the route that is now the A40" is more likely.

Our road – as patronized by our prehistoric ancestors. What a badge of honour! And what a shame that the information has only emerged since Harper made his journey. He'd have loved that detail.

The mountains' very presence means we need to make a decision. Route 47 skirts to the south of them, but Jim's modified route takes us north. I'll never know if it's easier on our muscles, but it's certainly easy on the eye. He's even managed to include another verdant and "mushroomy" valley, crossing the *Afon Brynberian* by way of a picturesque ford. Note: no long-distance bike ride is complete without at least one ford.

But, disorientated by his changes, I am keen to establish exactly where we are – and how far we have to go. So when a friendly dog walker seems to be equally up for explaining, I can't resist getting the map out of the pannier and spreading it out on the grass like a starchy-stiff picnic rug.

Dave has seen this before during my ride from London and Edinburgh. But it's a new one for the other two.

They glance at Dave, as if to say "What the…?"

Silently, with just hand signals and arched eyebrows, Dave does a fantastic job of conveying a message along the lines of, "Sometimes he gets like this. Just give him five minutes." To be fair, I make a reasonable fist of pretending I haven't seen him either.

Five minutes becomes ten as my new best mate and I get on our hands and knees to better explore the terrain. Ordnance Survey's Gothic script is littered across this landscape. As well as standing stones, there are chambered cairns and tumuli. While most of the national park hugs the coast, it's no surprise to see its borders extended inland here – protective arms wrapped around a sacred landscape.

It turns out that one particularly iconic site is close by. Extra cycling effort on an already tough day is a big ask, but I manage to persuade the others that Pentre Ifan will be worth it.

The lady – with her very patient dog – gets up, smiles and prepares to go on her way.

"*Pob lwc,*" she says.

Good luck.

———

Pentre Ifan is as visually spectacular as it is difficult to describe. Effectively one huge slab of flattish rock is balanced perhaps 8 feet in the air by three upright stones at one end and a single stone at the other. At first sight the arrangement looks precarious. But, as the interpretation board points out, they've stood this way for 5,000 years.

"*Carreg sy'n hofran*" runs the blurb's title: the floating stone.

The experts are convinced that this "elegant tripod" was built to impress in Neolithic times, but they can't agree on its precise purpose. A tomb, a landmark or "a dwelling place for supernatural beings" are among the options laid out for us.

Supernatural or not, it certainly has the wow factor. You turn off the road along a footpath accompanied by what I can only describe as a living wall – some sort of dry-stone construction long since over-run by all manner of flora. Occasionally an oversized stone either sticks out of it or lies within the grass – as though casually discarded by those ancient architects.

And then you see Pentre Ifan itself, set on sloping grassland with a tranquil and light blue sea in the distance. Its simplicity is disarmingly beautiful. If this were in a more populated part of the UK the stones would no doubt be a ring-fenced, paid-for attraction, complete with café and small museum.

Up here all we get is a lay-by with a capacity for half a dozen cars and a couple of basic metal bars to lock a bike to. I love a museum, I love a café, but I'm not arguing with this status quo.

———

Back on the road, Dave's bike is now causing him serious problems. Basically, the pedals won't always engage, leaving him spinning like crazy and getting nowhere. The only answer is the biking equivalent of the push start; racing along on foot until he reaches a high enough speed for it to kick in again.

We hold an emergency committee meeting at the top of the next hill.

"Can you make it, Dave?"

"Well, I've got to make it. What choice do I have?"

Nige is our go-to mechanic.

"Nige, what can you do?"

"His freewheel hub is knackered – the teeth are worn. You can't fix that on the road."

"Should a couple of us cycle off and find a bike shop?"

"What, round here? No chance. And anyway they wouldn't have the right part."

Silence fills the air.

Clearly there is no alternative. Dave has to either keep going however steep the hill or we need to be very patient if he gets off.

Thankfully, the landscape responds sympathetically. We're slow to realize that we're actually coming off the Preselis and descending into a valley, the Gwaun Valley. The worst of the climbing has to be over as barren moorland gets replaced with a chirpy little river shaded by compact trees drawing sustenance from richer soil on the valley floor. The very air tastes different. Sweet, lowland and water-tinged, not rougher, highland wafts. As the land becomes more furrowed, Dave's brow becomes less furrowed.

The Gwaun runs for just 10 miles between the mountains and the coast at Fishguard. Indeed, in Welsh, Fishguard is known as *Abergwaun*. And it doesn't take long for me to fall for it in much the same way as I did for the Windrush back in Oxfordshire.

In fact, it feels as if it's a world unto itself, a feeling reinforced by the charming *Hen Galan* tradition. *Hen Galan* translates as the Old New Year and dates back to 1752 when we switched to the Gregorian calendar.

The move "abolished" 11 days in September to realign the dates with the equinoxes, correcting a tiny annual discrepancy that had built up over the centuries. The change from the old Julian calendar had long since been adopted by other European countries, but on these isles we weren't happy. In England it even prompted the so-called Calendar Riots. In this corner of Wales they went for a more subtle protest – continuing to celebrate New Year on the old date of 13 January.

And they've kept going ever since. To this day residents go from house to house singing and being given sweets in return. The traditional song runs:

Blwyddyn Newydd dda i chi
Ac i bawb sydd yn y tŷ
Dyma fy nymuniad i
Blwyddyn Newydd dda i chi

The rhymes are lost in English, but it translates as:

A happy new year to you
And to everyone in the house
This is my wish
A happy new year to you.

To be so wilfully backward-looking might seem perverse, but honestly it all makes sense when you're cycling through. Houses are few and far between – the odd farmhouse here and there, that's it.

I also chance upon another beautiful church – the Jabes Baptist Chapel, smartly painted in doll's house shades of pale blue and white. It looks down over its own sloping graveyard and the wider valley, Romanesque in style rather than Carmarthen classical. For me, chapel architecture *is* Welsh architecture. I've been paying attention since Monmouth, admiring other examples on both lonely hilltops and busy town centres. Their sheer number is testimony to the immense religious enthusiasm of the nineteenth century. But here on the outskirts of the scattered village of Pontfaen I think I have found my most refined example yet.

Wales, I'm finding, likes to hide its jewels away, off the beaten track.

———

From about Crymych onwards I have been mentioning the prospect of a pint in the middle of nowhere at a pub with a stellar reputation. I detected scepticism from the others – perhaps over its very existence, certainly over the chances of it being open. But to everyone's delight the Dyffryn Arms is both close to Jabes Chapel and ready to welcome the thirsty cyclist.

Admittedly we almost ride past it without noticing. At first – and indeed second – glance it looks like a residential house; without as much as a hanging sign, let alone the usual paraphernalia of parasols and pub tables. But I guess this deadpan exterior makes sense because this place is as renowned for its lack of facilities as for the warmth of its welcome – no food, no wifi and only an outside loo.

Certainly, as we step across the threshold the decades roll away. You walk down a rather scruffy passageway thinking you may have entered the wrong building, before turning left into what looks like a period front room but is actually the main bar.

There's a small wood-burning stove against one wall, traditional wooden settles against two of the others and chequered quarry tiles on the floor. I put my yellow bike helmet down on a table, only to reflexively pick it up again because it looks so out of place; too bright, too modern – like an electric light switch on show in a Tudor drama.

Prints hang from wallpapered walls on brass picture hooks. And with the exception of the portrait of a young-looking Queen, nothing much would have looked out of place a century ago. Indeed the Queen's relatively recent death somehow adds to a sense of pleasantly bygone melancholia.

It takes me a while to realize that the reason the Dyffryn Arms looks "wrong" is because there is no bar. But, as we struggle to orientate ourselves, scuffled noises draw attention to a small hatch on the far wall. This, it turns out, is where the beer is to be found. And – 30 seconds later – a smiling barmaid too.

"Afternoon, lads. Welcome. What can I get you?"

We each have a pint of Bass served from the barrel via a jug, on the grounds that it's the only drink available – apart from a few bottles. Similarly we use cash because – guess what – there is no other way to pay. And anyway, at £3.30 a pint, who's arguing? As I wait for my change, I glance across at a small poster above the fireplace, imploring us to Drink More Bass. Well, it's difficult to do anything else.

I ask after Bessie, the legendary landlady whose family have owned the pub for 150 years. She began serving beer here in 1950 before taking it over in 1972. Sadly, we're told that she's not at all well. But the family link continues, we're being served by her granddaughter.[1]

---

1 A few months later, I read in the local press that Bessie Davies had died at the age of 93. Local councillor John Davies spoke to Wales Online about her no-nonsense style. When asked for a lager and lime by one visitor, she responded by saying "we don't do cocktails here". When another complained that the beer was cloudy she said "it's not cloudy, the glass is dirty" and gave it back to them. Most locals had already called the Dyffryn Arms "Bessie's" for years – and I doubt that will stop now.

Taking our drinks outside, I look above the door properly and notice that there is a sign, it's just that it looks more like a private house plate; low-key, like everything else.

I stretch out sore legs on a bench donated by the darts team in honour of Bessie's 75th birthday and, for the first time, allow myself to consider the finishing line. From London suburbs, through rounded Cotswold hills to the Welsh border and now a living museum of a pub quietly defying the twenty-first century; happy in its own world and perhaps its own calendar.

The Bass is going down very nicely and I resolve to appreciate every last second of the journey. Certainly the Dyffryn Arms joins the village of Windrush, St Peter's Church, Dixton and Pentre Ifan on my list of places with the kind of quixotic qualities that I can't adequately translate to the printed page.

Somehow our conversation slows down. This seat doesn't offer a view as such – a narrow lane, some sort of outbuilding and a hedge full of industrious sparrows. But it does offer an other-worldly tranquillity, a spot where you find yourself tuning in to the landscape, almost whether you like it or not.

———

Eventually we get back on the bikes and continue through the rest of this shaded arcadia. For a short while our road sits nicely above the Gwaun, meaning we're well-placed to spot a gaunt, grey heron, patrolling the shallows below. Later we cross it via a tiny bridge before it flows away across meadows to our right.

Jim – still the keeper of the Komoot flame – had promised that there would be no more hills between the Dyffryn Arms and Fishguard. This turns out to be wildly optimistic and he is roundly denounced for each and every climb on the 5 remaining miles.

The low point for me – in more ways than one – is a sign declaring a 20 per cent upward gradient. But this climb *is* the last, the reward being our first views of the pleasantly complicated coastline of *Bae Abergwaun* with the Pencaer Peninsula beyond. It also means we can see the broad sweep of our finishing line – and smell it in the salty air. At this distance I can start to make out Fishguard's constituent parts: the modern ferry port around Goodwick, Fishguard proper and the Lower Town where the Gwaun discharges itself into the sea. At one end, a long breakwater shows where the ferries set off for Ireland. At the other, everything appears on a smaller scale; cottages, a sheltered harbour and boats on swinging moorings.

I now have a throbbing calf muscle in my left leg – a particular kind of ache that only kicks in after the most arduous of days. But adrenalin will see me through from here – after all I started in the capital and am now on a Welsh coastline. I wouldn't say that my heart skips a beat, but there's a growing sense of satisfaction, even quiet elation. Even Dave's grumbling freewheel hub seems to realize that now is not the time to misbehave.

The outskirts of Fishguard soon follow, offering the unfamiliar sounds of suburbia: barking dogs, whirring lawn mowers, and then the sizzle of a fat fryer at a chippy. It's a busy place but you can't really get lost – both the road layout and gravity quickly draw us towards the market square, bathed in late afternoon sunlight.

Nige, Dave and Jim's eyes are immediately drawn to the Royal Oak; mine to the town hall, home to a well-regarded exhibition on the so-called "Last Invasion" of Britain back in 1797. It took place about 3 miles from here as the crow flies and, unexpectedly, we've made it about 20 minutes before museum closing time. I don't even attempt to convince them that a close examination of a tapestry detailing every detail of this historic clash should be top of their agenda. They turn right; I turn left.

Because even after a long day in the saddle I am keen to find out why more than 1,000 Frenchmen were invading British soil in the first place. And why on earth did they choose the obscure Carreg Wastad Point as the place to make landfall?

First, the context. We're talking about revolutionary France where a number of madcap schemes were given free rein. This particular plan involved trying to "export" the revolution to Ireland with the help of a much larger group of soldiers on board an armada of vessels. In the end, that incursion never happened – the ships were beaten back by bad weather. So, instead we're left looking at one of the diversionary raids aimed at confusing the enemy. A starter without the main course if you like. And an hors d'oeuvre which turned into a right horlicks.

The 1,400 men on board four ships were led by an American–Irishman called Colonel William Tate. He hated the English alright, but was hardly a military genius. And about half of his charges were actually criminals specially freed from French jails – expendable in the eyes of the authorities and the very opposite of a disciplined, fighting force.

Tate too had experienced bad luck with the weather. The initial plan was to attack Bristol, but the vagaries of the wind had driven them towards this Plan B. After all, the natives were poor and would be quick to rise up with revolutionary fervour against a hated elite, wouldn't they? What could possibly go wrong?

The Last Invasion Tapestry runs for 100 feet across the first floor of the town hall within what is now a library. I wait at the inquiry desk, pay my £3.50 and follow the assistant as she unlocks the door to allow me inside a subtly lit side-room.

Compiled by 77 women using 178 shades of wool, the tapestry is quite a feat of organization, creativity and historical acumen – an imaginative way to mark the 200th anniversary of the clash. An early panel shows a retired sailor standing on the headland spotting unfamiliar ships on the horizon with his telescope. Thomas Williams was among the first to realize the gravity of the situation. Word spread and soon there were dozens of people following the ships' progress around the coast, hearts no doubt in mouths.

Many of the invaders may have been criminals, but they were on board some of the most sophisticated ships of the time. Under cover of darkness the French navy managed to get them safely disembarked onto Welsh soil. Substantial amounts of arms made it too, together with 47 barrels of gunpowder. About 600 Grenadiers then established a beachhead and took over a nearby farm – decent enough progress. But the convicts were less easy to corral and command.

By sheer coincidence, a Portuguese ship had recently run aground, leaving a cargo of wine and port to be salvaged by opportunists. As a result, every cottage and farmhouse had a crate or two of booze invitingly within reach. Revolutionary fighting fervour dissolved with the pop of every cork – and one of the panels on the tapestry shows legless Frenchmen rolling around on the ground.

But at this stage the local authorities didn't know that. And in an era when information could only travel as fast as a messenger on horseback, they had to think for themselves and prepare to fight for their lives too. The logistical difficulties of getting enough men in the right place provided the leaders with a real headache – and there were also arguments over who should take command.

The resolve of the poor, the cowardice of the rich – who largely fled – and the imperfect but understandable decisions made by those in charge are well-told by Phil Carradice in his book *Britain's Last Invasion*.

And, as the tapestry makes clear, a combination of French drunkenness and Welsh bluff (giving the impression they had more troops than they did) ended up in unconditional surrender. Two days after they landed, the Frenchmen were lined up on Goodwick Sands, ignominiously throwing their weapons in a pile and being taken into custody as breathless locals looked on.

At one level it was a pathetic, half-baked plan, doomed to failure. But as word of "invasion" spread, it was enough to prompt a run on the pound in London. Ultimately, it led the authorities to establish a much more rigorous set of coastal defences including the so-called Martello Towers that stretch all the way along the south and east coast of England. The most northerly one is at Aldeburgh in Suffolk where my wife's family hail from. I wonder how many people there know about the invasion 375 miles to the west which prompted its construction.

I say thank you to the staff for their patience (it's a tad past the official closing time…) and head to the Royal Oak. Looking above the front door, I notice a sign saying

"Last Invasion of Britain Peace Treaty Was Signed Here in 1797". Clearly the other three have been engaged in their own detailed research.

At the bar I can't resist buying a pint of Jemima's Pitchfork in honour of Jemima Nicholas, a brawny cobbler who is said to have captured 12 French soldiers single-handedly. Of course, this is far too good a story to worry about precise historical accuracy and a memorial stone in her honour lies next door in the churchyard with "The Welsh Heroine" proudly inscribed upon it.

The Royal Oak has a spacious beer garden looking directly down on the Lower Town and the mouth of the *Afon Gwaun*.

"So this will do as the finishing line, won't it, Steve?" says Jim, pint in hand.

"Here? No way. We've got to make it down to that harbour," I reply, the final scene already well-choreographed in my head.

"What, down that really steep hill that we'll then have to cycle up again."

"That's the one."

The slope is indeed steep, but the setting is scenic – and undeniably *Welsh*. No wonder they set the TV version of Dylan Thomas's *Under Milk Wood* here. A closer look at the Google map even reveals something called "Richard Burton's Famous Viewpoint" on high ground above, in memory of the actor's spine-tingling performance.

We freewheel down Hill Terrace, the full shape of the compact harbour revealing itself as we descend. The sun has never really got out today and the sky is overcast, perhaps that smudge close to the horizon is light rain in St George's Channel.

But within the sheltered harbour, the water is unruffled and crystal clear. Here, there's more than enough room for 20-odd boats to lie moored up, their bows facing out to sea. On the far side, my eye is also drawn to half a dozen terraced cottages painted in pastel shades, their creams, blues and pinks imperfectly reflected in the shallows beneath. Beyond, a walled road climbs steeply above their back gardens before winding around the next headland. In Wales there is always another hill to climb, another summit to conquer.

A 20 mph sign welcomes us to Cwm Abergwaun – Lower Town – where we re-cross the Gwaun just before it completes its journey. A couple of tight corners must be a nightmare for lorry drivers but we find Quay Street and get off the bikes next to a sculpture called *Fishguard Herrings*. A tight shoal of metallic fish swims busily through the sky, the sculpture attached to a rock that turns out to be a Preseli bluestone. This will do then, this will definitely do. Later, we will make our way back up the steep slope before realizing that our Airbnb is an annoying 2 miles further on. Dave's final composition will also be revealed – a poem of rain and pain, a bard and Fishguard, a long ride and no little pride. Most controversially, the Welsh pronunciation of *Cymru* will somehow be married to the Norfolk pronunciation of "homely". All so excruciating that it is somehow brilliant.

But for now we line up, bikes facing the camera for the group photo. Low tide and hilly cliffs in the distance, big smiles and aching limbs in the foreground. This has been my kind of holiday, my kind of cycling, my kind of adventure. From central London to the Welsh coast – Monday to Monday – under my own steam.

———

The last time I completed one of these long-distance trips I had the odd downer as well as the highs. This time, I can honestly say it's all been good. Previous experience probably helps – I know when to push my body and when to take it easy. The breathtaking quality of the landscape can't have done any harm either. But most importantly, I've been on my own for less of the journey. Certainly for the tougher stretches, I've had others with whom to share my thoughts – as well as pints of Jemima's Pitchfork. That's the key to cycle touring, I decide: find some good friends and do it together. A ride shared is a mileage halved.

A fourth "friend" died a long time ago after making the same journey on a much more basic machine. He too had spent his time scribbling away, trying to sum up the different shades of England and Wales that he'd found along the way. Another two-wheeled quest with a serene finishing line.

Charles G. Harper, a selfie might have confused you, so we decided upon a more traditional photo. And this one's for you.

Steve, Dave, Nige and Jim

HIGHWAYS
AND BYWAYS
– MY ROUTE

I enjoyed using St Paul's as my starting line. The building itself provides the iconic location, but the unshowy churchyard to the rear allows enough anonymity for quiet, last-minute preparations.

From there I followed the route of the A40 as far as Marble Arch. The modern road then veers north via a short stretch of the A5 as far as Westway where it re-establishes its own identity – elevated dual carriageways and all.

Westway did tempt me. After all, there is a story to be told about how controversial the road was when it was proposed and built in the late 1960s. Local people felt that working class communities were being sacrificed on the altar of automotive heaven. There are some juicy cultural references too – The Clash, The Jam and Pete Doherty have all either sung about it or posed beneath it. Big names.

But I had this feeling that Charles Harper wouldn't have approved – on geographical as much as musical grounds. So I stuck to the main drag as he knew it – effectively the Uxbridge Road. This route – now re-classified as the A4020 – remains mostly un-dualled and is much more suited to a cyclist's needs. A look at any London map will show it minding its own business, sandwiched between the showier A4 to the south and the "new" A40 to the north.

I diverted – briefly – to the Grand Union Canal at Hanwell and even entertained thoughts of sticking with the towpath all the way to Uxbridge. If a friendly boater had offered, I may even have hitched a lift – after all there's nothing like a bit of gongoozling to make you forget that you're in the big city. Having said that, I never felt remotely unsafe as a cyclist within Greater London. The capital has made great strides on this front in recent years.

Things get trickier beyond the M25 with the A40 becoming particularly unfriendly for cyclists between Denham and Beaconsfield. I was unable to find any safer alternatives in these parts. Cycle lanes are desperately needed.

Wycombe was welcoming while the route around and beyond the separate village of West Wycombe was manageable. At Piddington not everyone will want to be so wilfully historical, but in any event the turnpike road provides a ready alternative for people who prefer tarmac to a muddy track. (But Bottom Wood – alongside that track – is rightly considered a jewel in the Chiltern Society's crown.)

Cycling through Oxford was of course a joy – although the decent facilities quickly disappear in its western suburbs. All power to the people fighting for a dedicated cycle path through Botley and on to Eynsham. More details of their campaign can be found on the www.b4044path.org website.

My Day Three was all about getting into the Cotswolds proper. And while the A40 does become increasingly busy, there were always inviting alternatives most of which shadowed the River Windrush. Unsurprisingly, these pretty, hedgerow-lined lanes and accompanying villages were well-used by cyclists – everyone from head-down MAMILS to meandering holidaymakers. I hope that I was more the latter than the former.

Beyond Northleach, I guess you could take the A40 itself, but I didn't fancy it. There are alternatives via Cheltenham as well as the hotchpotch of roads that I hit upon. Mile for mile, I don't think I could have extracted much more from the Cotswolds. Despite the gradients, I was very happy with the choices I made. In addition to the gorgeous scenery, it was peaceful – I came across very few cars on these lonesome lanes.

My route towards Gloucester included the beginnings of a massive road-building programme to its east – it's what National Highways calls the "A417 Missing Link". I hope that this expensive and ambitious project will make life easier for cyclists as well as cars. It's due for completion in 2027. But despite all the expensive, fly-through videos on the website, I will always prefer the precipitous Birdlip Hill as my gateway to Gloucester – even though it's not for the faint-hearted. The remaining miles into this chilled-out city were straightforward.

Cycle paths west from Gloucester get you to the village of Over very safely and scenically. Beyond, the A40 is manageable but not ideal. As in Buckinghamshire, I occasionally played safe and rode on the pavement rather than mix it with motor traffic.

I decided to turn off the main road at Huntley on the spur of the moment – but subsequent road trips made me realize I'd made the right choice. Ross-on-Wye might be a lovely town, but several stretches of the A40 beyond Huntley wouldn't have been much fun. I later learned that the great road engineer Thomas Telford had planned to re-route the main road to Wales roughly along the line I took through the Forest of Dean. I felt vindicated, even if the rise of the railways meant that his ideas never saw the light of day.

My most egregious mistake of the whole trip happened to the north of Monmouth. I was guilty of wishful thinking here, assuming I could busk my way alongside the A40, unaware that it's virtually a motorway in these parts. So when I pitched up at Whitchurch, I had already made some wrong decisions. By far the best way for the cyclist is via Symonds Yat, picking up the Peregrine Path which runs along the banks of the Wye. The Sustrans website has a dedicated page for this 7½-mile route. Either way please don't do what I did. It was neither big nor clever. It is also probably the worst way for a cyclist to cross from England into Wales across the entire 160-mile-long border.

From Monmouth – where I joined Nige, Dave and Jim – we stayed north of the A40 as far as Raglan before dipping to the south beyond. From there on, it was all about crossing the River Usk as early as possible to allow us to reach the sanctuary of the Monmouth and Brecon canal. The Mon and Brec effectively meant we could forget about navigation for about 25 miles. Having said that, Heron Maps do an excellent chart covering the entire canal – complete with extra information and photographs. (Their Grand Union equivalent for the London area is also worth having.)

From Brecon onwards, we were forced to the north of the main road and climbed hundreds of extra feet in the process. I would love to see cycle paths in the Usk valley here – I don't think it would take much to persuade more people to explore this inviting part of Wales on two wheels rather than four.

I chose to take the Roman road to Llandovery simply because it was the oldest route available and I fancied the challenge. You don't have to be a hardcore cyclist to enjoy it – although you definitely need a mountain bike.

The A4069 and then the Bethlehem Road provided the perfect alternative to the A40 all the way down to Llandeilo – and the views across the Tywi valley are superb. Similarly the B4300 did the same job to Carmarthen with a minimum of fuss.

And then there was our final day. Initially I was torn between Fishguard as the ultimate destination and Milford Haven – the end of the line for Charles Harper back in 1905. But everyone I spoke to recommended Fishguard – thanks in particular to Mike Parker, Marc P. Jones and Andrew Chapman. This prompted the next question: could I get to Fishguard by shadowing the A40? Well, there are fragments of the older road around Bancyfelin and St Clears as well as decent stretches to the east of Whitland. But they would have been punctuated by nasty bouts of main-road-itis. With four of us travelling as a mini-peloton, I just didn't fancy it.

All of which led us to the hilly joys of Route 47 on the National Cycle Network. We soon discovered why the main road takes the long way round. But the sense of achievement was enormous and the Gwaun Valley provides the perfect gateway to the coast.

We called it a day there. But if you really want to Go West, there's always the ferry to Ireland. Perhaps this trip is really just the appetizer for Rosslare, County Wexford and beyond. Perhaps every journey is just a prequel for the road yet to be travelled.

GO *WEST* – DAY TRIPS

Not everyone has the time to put together an eight-day excursion, but everyone should get out more. Here are some ideas for shorter rides, walks and a paddle – day by day.

Day One – Colne Valley Regional Park

London falls away quickly on its north western border, with the River Colne, the Grand Union Canal and the M25 conspiring to contain the capital. When seen from the motorway, it might seem an unlikely spot for recreation but a "regional park" has nevertheless been created – plenty of green space and a bewildering variety of waterways, lakes and reservoirs. It runs to 43 square miles in all, encompassing parts of Hertfordshire, Buckinghamshire, Berkshire and Surrey as well as the borough of Hillingdon. In many ways this isn't "natural nature" – most of the reservoirs were a twentieth-century response to London's population explosion, while several of the lakes are old gravel pits. Still, it offers people a handy sanctuary from bus routes and exhaust fumes. More oystercatcher than Oyster card.

Using Denham Country Park as a base, you quickly discover the rivers Misbourne, Colne and Frays jostling for space with the Grand Union. But be warned that some of the tracks are footpaths rather than cycle-friendly bridleways. Slightly further afield, the 7-mile Colne Valley Trail *is* a bike route linking Uxbridge to Rickmansworth while a footpath connects the park to the village of Denham – complete with a number of tempting pubs along its high street.

Denham is arguably the first genuine village the cyclist encounters in this direction out of London. I have a particular soft spot for The Green Man pub after first coming across it on the last day before a winter Covid lockdown. Perhaps it was that sense of impending incarceration that made me appreciate its virtues. Five hand-pulled pumps at the bar, open brickwork behind. Seven bearded millennials were knocking back their lager in quiet defiance of the "rule of six" guidelines. And there was that special kind of laughter that accompanies a good joke well-told. I remember sitting on my own with a pint of Rebellion Smuggler, quietly registering that the gag would neither be delivered nor received quite so raucously in any other setting than a British boozer. Recommended.

Day Two – Eynsham and Witney

Eynsham is a welcoming village lying just beyond the Oxford hinterland. It was once home to an abbey, still has a smart "market house" building and harbours ambitions for a museum. I barely scratched the surface during my visit, but its history is well laid out on the parish council's website.

For cyclists, I recommend a circular route from Eynsham to Witney returning via the village of Stanton Harcourt. For the first few miles you can shadow the route I took on Day Three, leaving Eynsham via Mill Street and then using pavements alongside the A40 as far as Oxford Hill. On leaving Witney perhaps drop in on the "living museum" of Cogges Manor Farm. The "living" bit means you get to trip up over free range hens and admire sheep and goats as well as more traditional historic attractions. The building itself dates back to the thirteenth century and might feel familiar to *Downton Abbey* fans because it was used as the farmhouse where Lady Edith's illegitimate daughter was brought up by a farming couple – with all of the class-ridden angst the drama depicts so well.

The grounds of Cogges Manor are extensive – a sheltered orchard here, lazy meadows there. In between, a wooden play fort stands on the site of a small castle, probably built to protect a ford across the River Windrush. Before Witney's bridge was built in the early thirteenth century, Cogges provided the shallowest place to cross the river in these parts. As the accompanying blurb says, "in more than 1,000 years the route has shifted by only about 500 metres".

From Cogges, find the very quiet but badly maintained single track road to Stanton Harcourt – hybrid or mountain bikes would be best. One look at the map will show you that the lane threads its way through a mosaic of pools and lagoons – mostly flooded gravel pits now converted into "fisheries". But, at least in summer, all hints of water are concealed by thick hedgerows on either side. Later, make sure you cycle through the village of Stanton Harcourt rather than accidentally taking the bypass. The last 3 miles to Eynsham are admittedly on a busier, narrower B-road than is ideal.

Accommodation-wise, I am a big fan of The Talbot Inn in Eynsham – at least partially because I'm not sure I've ever stayed at a pub with a "wharfside terrace" before. Both the food and the beer were excellent and of course you get much better value than you would in tourist-centred Oxford. The inn lies on the village's outskirts, close to Swinford Toll Bridge.

Day Three – Burford
As you may have noticed, I loved Burford. And there was so much to say about the town that I couldn't really do justice to the legends surrounding the nearby Wychwood Forest – much reduced in size since its medieval heyday.

So, for a quick Wychwood–Windrush tour, grab a bike and head north along the high street, cross the bridge and turn right at the T-junction. You then climb Fulbrook Hill

– a steepish climb towards the sparsely populated high ground which separates the Windrush valley from that of the Evenlode. This neck of the woods was once home to the notorious Dunsdon brothers – highwaymen who preyed on travellers passing through Wychwood. Tom, Dick and Harry – no, really – worked together until Dick lost his arm during a bungled burglary, and was never to be seen again. But Tom and Harry continued to terrorize the district until 1784 when they were finally hanged in Gloucester for their crimes. Their bodies were taken back to their old patch to be gibbeted – in other words hung from a prominent landmark as a gruesome deterrent, a common form of post-death humiliation for highwaymen.

In this case the landmark was a tree and amazingly it's still there, albeit on private land. I believe it to be the most northerly of the four oaks that you can see from the main road just beyond Shipton Downs Farm. Apparently trespassers can see the initials TD carved into the bark.

The road out of Fulbrook is busy, so it's a relief to turn left at the next crossroads onto a single-track lane signposted to Downs Lodge Farm. Admire the cherry trees in the hedgerow and continue south west. This road is on a ridge and soon offers fantastic views to both north and the south – for miles and miles to the south in fact.

Keep left and then turn right at a double junction before proceeding to a crossroads with the main Burford to Stow-on-the-Wold road. Go straight over onto a battered old lane which descends to Taynton – a village which has links to the Strong family of stonemasons who I mention in my account of Day Three.

Turn right at the next junction to cycle through Taynton itself, enjoying the wealth of detail in the houses' honeycomb-coloured stone. The gardens are pretty too. The road then rises and falls as it heads west to slightly larger Great Barrington – note the slightly greyer tone of the stone here.

Keep left at the war memorial and descend towards the River Windrush, passing the grand entrance to Barrington Park, complete with gratuitously high walls. Cross the river, pass The Fox Inn and then climb again towards the houses clustered around the greened-over quarry site in the middle of Little Barrington. Turn left towards the top of this dip to pass the church. You're now returning to Burford along the same narrow lane that I took in the other direction.

Day Four – Gloucester

It's clear that the only place to stay in Gloucester is the galleried New Inn, for all that it could do with a bit of a twenty-first-century makeover. As for the city, the big surprise for me was the wealth of history around the docks – well-chronicled in the nearby National Waterways Museum.

So if the swooping aerial shots of the Gloucester to Sharpness Canal on the museum videos whet your appetite, either walk or cycle the Towpath Trail alongside. This waterway is a proper ship canal rather than the much narrower examples I enjoyed on both the outskirts of London and clinging to the side of that Monmouthshire hill. In fact, it was the biggest canal in England when it was opened in 1827 – 86 feet 6 inches wide and 18 feet deep.

The going along this 16-mile stretch is easy with a decent quality surface. I particularly enjoyed the hustle and bustle around Saul Junction – approximately halfway along the route. It is that rare thing, a canal crossroads – intersecting with the Stroudwater Canal, connecting the town of Stroud to the Severn. Here, there are still boatyards and cranes as well as refreshments and a visitor centre.

Look out for the two pleasure boats operated by The Willow Trust and specially adapted to allow disabled people to enjoy regular cruises.

Day Five – The River Wye

Our Day Five was spent on the Wye and we can't praise Monmouth Canoes enough. Their yard lies on the Old Dixton Road, opposite the town's leisure centre. We hired two Canadian canoes and paid extra for Guide Nigel – whose expertise was invaluable. Their team will transport you and the canoes up to Kerne Bridge, allowing you to make your own way back on the water. The day runs from 8.30 a.m. to 4 p.m. On our stretch of river there was also a half-day option starting at Huntsham Bridge, much nearer to Symonds Yat. But the company's longest trip runs from Hay-on-Wye to Monmouth – that's 80 miles across five or six days. More details at www.monmouthcanoe.co.uk.

Day Six – Dingestow

A little beyond Monmouth, look out for the so-called Tread and Trot route known as "Dingestow Discoveries" online. This runs to 5½ miles and is suitable for walkers, horse riders and mountain bikers. It loops north from the village of Dingestow as far as Offa's Dyke – the great ditch which once separated King Offa's kingdom of Mercia from the Welsh lands beyond.

The walk starts close to the Bridge Caravan Park and Camping Site in Dingestow. Walk towards the river and take the first on the left, not the track to Mill Farm, but the bridleway sign through a wood. You might recall me saying that the old house at the site was once a coaching inn on the Monmouth to Raglan route. According to the T&T leaflet, nearby Jingle Street is so-called because of the sound the bells made on the horses' harnesses.

We stayed at The King's Head in Monmouth – another former coaching inn. This one dates back to the seventeenth century and boasts of a visit by Charles I during the English Civil War. More recently it was given a makeover and, as ever with Wetherspoons, the job was done thoroughly. The historically minded will find prints and texts in honour of famous visitors and locals – everyone from Geoffrey of

Monmouth to Henry V. Don't miss the ornate ceiling in the King's Room. Upstairs, the hotel bedrooms have been refurbished to a high standard and our bikes were securely locked away by helpful staff.

Day Seven – Llandovery and Carmarthen
An off-road bike track from Llandeilo to Carmarthen along the route of an old railway track is due to open in autumn 2025. Badged as the Tywi Valley Path, it won more than £16 million from various arms of government. The major works include two new bridges. Carmarthen County Council sees this 16-mile trail as being a key part of its mission to become the "Cycling hub of Wales".

Llandovery remains the most atmospheric place to stay for the night and I recommend The King's Head in the heart of the town centre. This inn was famously once home to the Bank of the Black Ox – set up to help drovers safeguard the large amounts of money that ebbed to and fro with the livestock. It was established in 1799 by David Jones. He'd worked there as a lad, regularly overhearing the farmers asking the landlord for help in keeping their money safe.

Initially, his system worked on the principle that the famous Black Ox bank notes weren't general currency – they could only be exchanged by stockmen who all knew each other. The failproof nature of this scheme is illustrated by a story contained on a rather tatty sheet of laminated A4 pinned to a wall, right at the back of the pub. Apparently in the old days the special bank notes could occasionally be found wedged into the walls of London's less salubrious guesthouses. Why? Because they'd been stolen – along with any cash – from the drovers' trousers by light-fingered prostitutes but were then hidden because the women knew they were worthless – and incriminating.

Llandovery is very proud of its links with these stockmen. Llandovery Rugby Club are nicknamed The Drovers and don't miss the statue of a big-booted, greatcoat-wearing drover staring rather beadily at you as you pass the museum.

Talking of drovers, the county council has designed a so-called Wild Drovers' Way for those who prefer to tour by car. Allow three to four days for this 180-mile loop. The route offers the National Wool Museum, old gold mines, castles and the home of Dylan Thomas as well as plenty of "Carmarthen's lazy lanes".

Day Eight – Fishguard

In Fishguard I was sorely tempted by the Last Invasion Trail. This 18-mile cycling route starts at the Harbour Village Car Park in Goodwick and includes the beach where the French surrendered and many of the paths and properties used by both defenders and invaders. It's one of 26 trails on Pembrokeshire County Council's website, including others that focus on the Gwaun Valley, the Preseli Stones and Crymych. An impressive range.

But in the end I went for a straightforward walk from the church at Llanwnda to the very spot where the Frenchmen first made landfall – the spot is marked by a memorial stone installed on the 100th anniversary of that moment.

St Gwyndaf's was where some of the French soldiers sheltered, infamously using the pages of a seventeenth-century bible to try to start their fire. (According to The Last Invasion Tapestry they ransacked the church and burned manuscripts, which might be a harsh interpretation.) Either way, the remains are now on display in a sealed cabinet, having only been rediscovered within this atmospheric building as recently as the 1990s.

From there, you won't find a sign to the memorial stone, but stay to the left of the church and you'll soon pick up a path that runs towards the headland and the coast beyond. You're mostly walking across sheep pasture, but there is one narrow fern-infested path that I like to think the soldiers used as cover as they got to grips with a foreign land. Our route then meets the Pembrokeshire Coastal Path. Turn left to descend into a wooded valley, crossing a stream and then climbing towards heathland that can be alive with the purple of heather and the yellow of gorse at the right time of year.

The memorial stands strong and tall, but it's rather difficult to make out the words inscribed within it. Perhaps it's more important to look out across the narrow bay of Carreg Wastad. There's one small, shale-grey beach at the centre of the beach's horseshoe and, in my mind at least, this is where the rowing boats disgorged their passengers.

Afterwards go for a drink at The Ship Inn in Fishguard. This pub lies in the heart of the Lower Town and, apart from its old-fashioned nature and nautical theme, I recommend it because of a conversation I enjoyed there a week before my bike ride began.

It had started very much in English with a couple, perhaps in their early 60s, chatting to three younger men. Two of them then wandered off, leaving the third shooting the breeze. He admitted that his first language was Welsh. The couple responded enthusiastically and they made the linguistic switch. To my untutored ear, this was a fluent conversation, for all that it was punctuated by the odd "How do you say..." in apologetic English.

What cheered me most was the generous give and take. This was no purist lesson. It was three people conversing in the ancient language as best they could, in an increasingly Anglophone world. And their best seemed – to me at least – to be at least 95 per cent there.

I was itching to join in the conversation and eventually worked up the courage when the other two lads returned to the fray, one regretting that he hadn't listened more closely to his old Welsh-speaking nan.

I dived in, declared myself an Englishman and said I was on the nursery slopes of Welsh but with only a Duolingo streak to show for it. The older chap, it turned out, had returned to Wales in his 30s and decided that it was now or never. His other half was a North Walian; Welsh was her first language.

My Welsh is all but non-existent – a motley collection of nouns and the odd sorry sentence. But it was enough to prompt the older chap to say: "See, there's an English fella here trying to learn it. What's your excuse now?"

It was delivered with just the right mix of seriousness and levity.

"Use it or lose it, lads. Use it or lose it."

It was one conversation in one pub. But I think it bodes well for the future of the Welsh language.

ACKNOWLEDGEMENTS

A massive thank you to my wife, Debbie, for her love, patience, understanding and wise counsel all the way through. Thanks too, to our girls, Abbie and Maya, for chipping in with suggestions.

Thanks to my sister, Caroline, for her fantastic proofreading skills as well as her research within the magical world of local newspaper archives. And thanks to everyone else in my family – Dad, Colin, Martin and Katrina – for letting me bang on about niche historical topics at regular intervals.

On the road, the Loddon Mountain Bike Club (Without the Mountains) provided fantastic support from Day Five through to Day Eight. In addition, Jim Stuart was the most chilled of roomies, Nige Hampson rules the roost as club mechanic and Dave Matthews is unchallenged as poet laureate. Dave Fearns and Andy Colman drove all the way to Monmouth just for the weekend bants while Glyn and Maureen Matthews provided Welsh heritage expertise over dinner in Monmouth.

Finally I am very grateful to the Airbnb host in Potters Bar who told me, unbidden, that "Oxford Street" was a rubbish name for this book and that I should call it "Go West" instead. He was right.

At Summersdale, huge thanks to Siobhan Coleman for carefully shepherding the book through from manuscript to publication, and also to structural editor Ross Dickinson for suggesting dozens and dozens of helpful and wise improvements. In addition, copyeditor Kay Coleman's meticulousness saved me from serious embarrassment on several occasions. This book is immeasurably better for their contributions, but any errors are my own.

ABOUT THE AUTHOR

Steve Silk is a journalist with over 30 years' experience in TV and print. He is currently an Assistant Editor with BBC Look East in Norwich, producing the evening news programme.

He has previously worked as a TV reporter for *ITV News Anglia* and ITN *5 News*, where he covered everything from terrorist atrocities to Wembley cup finals. Before that he was a newspaper reporter for the *Norwich Evening News*, the Newcastle-based *Sunday Sun* and the *Darlington and Stockton Times*. But his favourite byline remains a front-page story for *The Times of India* in 1996 – a profile piece on The Barmy Army cricket fans.

Go West is his second cycling adventure. His first, *The Great North Road*, saw him ride from London to Edinburgh across 11 days. It was published by Summersdale in 2021.

He has also written books about Norfolk where he lives with his wife Debbie and their daughters Abbie and Maya. *The Wherryman's Way* (2010) won the East Anglian Travel Book of the Year. *Hidden Riverside Norwich* followed in 2016.

You can find him on social media @stevesilk66.

Photo by Jim Stuart

SELECT BIBLIOGRAPHY

Ayerst, David, *A History of Burford Church* (1975, Windrush Group)

Barber, Chris, *Hill's Tramroad: Blaenavon World Heritage Site* (2019, Amberley Publishing)

Bradley, Simon and others, *Oxfordshire: Oxford and the South East* (2023, Yale University Press)

Brill, Edith, *Portrait of the Cotswolds* (1964, Robert Hale)

Campbell, James W. P., *Building St Paul's* (2020, Thames & Hudson)

Carradice, Phil, *Britain's Last Invasion* (2020, Pen and Sword History)

Cauvain, Stanley, and others, *The Rye High Wycombe, A Priceless Possession* (1999, High Wycombe Society)

Chambers, Jill, *Buckinghamshire Machine Breakers* (1991, J. Chambers)

Child, Mark, *The Windrush Valley* (2013, Amberley Publishing)

Crane, Nicholas, *Great British Journeys* (2008, Weidenfeld & Nicolson)

Elias, Twm, *On the Trail of the Welsh Drovers* (2018, Gwasg Carreg Gwalch)

Emmerson, Andrew and Bancroft, Peter, *A, B, C and M: Road Numbering Revealed* (2007, Capital History)

Friends of Dixton Church, *Welcome to St Peter's Dixton* (booklet – Clarke Printing, Monmouth)

Grigg, Dr Russell, *The Little Book of Carmarthenshire* (2015, The History Press)

Harper, Charles G., *The Oxford, Gloucester and Milford Haven Road – Volume I* (1905, Chapman & Hall)

Harper, Charles G., *The Oxford, Gloucester and Milford Haven Road – Volume II* (1905, Chapman & Hall)

Humphreys, Alastair, *Ask an Adventurer* (2021, Eye Books)

Keighley, Charles, *Discovering Wychwood* (2000, Wychwood Press)

Kightly, Charles, *Chieftains and Princes* (1994, Cadw, Welsh Historic Monuments)

Lorie, Jonathan, *The Travel Writer's Way* (2019, Bradt Guides)

Mayes, L. J., *The History of Chairmaking in High Wycombe* (1960, Routledge & Kegan Paul)

Morris, Jan, *Wales: Epic Views of a Small Country* (2000, Penguin Books)

Oates, Jonathan, *Southall and Hanwell* (2002, Tempus Publishing)

Oates, Jonathan, *Acton: A History* (2008, Phillimore)

Parker, Mike, *All the Wide Border* (2023, Harper North)

Pevsner, Elizabeth and Nikolaus, *Buckinghamshire* (1994, Yale University Press)

Roberts, Iestyn, *William Williams: Pantycelyn* (2004, Gomer)

Taylor, A. J., *Minster Lovell Hall* (1985, English Heritage)

The Physicians of Myddfai Society, *The Physicians of Myddfai, A Continuing Tradition* (2022, The Physicians of Myddfai)

Thomas, Dylan, *Under Milk Wood* (1954, Phoenix)

Timpson, John, *Timpson's Timepaths* (1994, BBC Books)

Toulson, Shirley, *The Drovers* (1980, Shire Publications)

Turner, Joanna, *Quarries and Craftsmen of the Windrush Valley* (1988, Burford and District Society)

Verey, David and others, *Gloucestershire 1: The Cotswolds* (1999, Yale University Press)

Verey, David and Brooks, Alan, *Gloucestershire 2: The Vale and the Forest of Dean* (2002, Yale University Press)

"Annoyingly good" Tim Moore

THE GREAT NORTH ROAD

LONDON TO EDINBURGH
11 DAYS, 2 WHEELS AND 1 ANCIENT HIGHWAY

STEVE SILK

THE GREAT NORTH ROAD

Steve Silk

Paperback | ISBN: 978-1-80007-049-3

**The Great North Road is Britain's Route 66 –
we've just forgotten how to sing its praises**

In 1921, Britain's most illustrious highway, the Great
North Road, ceased to exist – on paper at least. Stretching
from London to Edinburgh, the old road was largely
replaced by the A1 as the era of the motor car took hold.

A hundred years later, journalist and cyclist Steve Silk
embraces the anniversary as the perfect excuse to set off
on an adventure across 11 days and 400 miles.

Travelling by bike at a stately 14 miles per hour, he heads
north, searching out milestones and memories, coaching
inns and coffee shops. Seen from a saddle rather than a
car seat, the towns and the countryside of England and
Scotland reveal traces of Britain's remarkable past and
glimpses of its future.

Enriched with history, humour and insight, *The Great
North Road* is a tribute to Britain and the endless appeal
of the open road.

Have you enjoyed this book?
If so, why not write a review on your favourite website?

If you're interested in finding out
more about our books, find us on Facebook
at **Summersdale Publishers**, on Twitter/X at
@Summersdale and on Instagram and TikTok
at **@summersdalebooks** and get in touch.
We'd love to hear from you!

Thanks very much for buying this Summersdale book.

www.summersdale.com